asian

HOMESTYLE

asian

bay books

contents

Incredible Asian cuisine

Asia. The very word conjures up visions of saffron-robed monks, lush jungles, brilliant-green rice paddies and cultures rich in tradition and colour. This continent is exotic, distinctive and completely alluring, and while we may not ever be fortunate enough to travel there, we can bring a little of it to life in our kitchens.

From curry to California rolls, noodles to nasi goreng and tandoori lamb to tempura, the textures and tastes of Asian cuisines have completely seduced modern cooks. We love the spicy sizzle of satay, the complex savour of a simmering hot-pot and the smoky drama of cooking in a wok. The pleasant heat of chilli in a dish quickly becomes addictive and the bright tang of lemongrass, ginger, lime and coriander are simply irresistible.

Because Asia is comprised of a diverse collection of countries, its cuisine is incredibly varied, with everything from delicate, fragrant salads, chewy, meaty dumplings, flaky flat-breads and robust, zesty braises found within its culinary borders. However, no matter whether a dish is Sri Lankan, Vietnamese, Japanese or Mongolian in origin, certain common threads run through all Asian cookery.

Dishes are, in the main, healthy and fresh, utilising vegetables, lean meats and other good ingredients to great effect. Some of these (yoghurt, sago, eggplant, sesame seeds) will already be known to most cooks but some will not. If miso, kecap manis, won ton wrappers or fish sauce, for example, are initially unfamiliar, a visit to an Asian food store (an interesting quest in itself for any cook) will quickly prove educational. Cooking methods are instantly recognisable, with frying, stir-frying, steaming, poaching, simmering and braising used widely in Asian cuisine.

Many supermarkets now stock Asian basics too, making it easy to find almost everything needed to create all the delicious recipes in this book. From the simplest of starters (Thai potato cakes or spring rolls) to sublimely sweet endings (caramel sticky rice), cooking Asian is a delicious adventure, and, armed with *Homestyle Asian*, it's one you'll want to embark on regularly.

Soups

Seafood laksa

PREPARATION TIME: 45 MINUTES | TOTAL COOKING TIME: 45 MINUTES | SERVES 4–6

1 kg (2 lb 4 oz) raw prawns (shrimp)

125 ml (4 fl oz/½ cup) oil

2–6 red chillies, seeded

1 onion, roughly chopped

3 garlic cloves, halved

2 cm (¾ inch) piece fresh ginger or galangal, quartered

1 teaspoon ground turmeric

1 tablespoon ground coriander

3 lemongrass stems, white part only, chopped

1–2 teaspoons shrimp paste

600 ml (21 fl oz) coconut cream

2 teaspoons grated palm sugar (jaggery)

4 makrut (kaffir lime) leaves

200 g (7 oz) packet fish balls

190 g (6¾ oz) packet fried bean curd pieces

250 g (9 oz) fresh thin egg noodles

250 g (9 oz) bean sprouts

1 very large handful mint, chopped, to serve

1 medium handful coriander (cilantro) leaves, to serve

NUTRITION PER SERVE (6)
Protein 50 g; Fat 50 g; Carbohydrate 40 g; Dietary Fibre 8 g; Cholesterol 270 mg; 3340 kJ (800 Cal)

1 Peel and devein the prawns, keeping the shells, heads and tails.

2 To make the prawn stock, heat 2 tablespoons of the oil in a large, heavy-based saucepan and add the prawn shells, heads and tails. Stir until the heads are bright orange, then add 1 litre (35 fl oz/4 cups) water. Bring to the boil, reduce the heat and simmer for 15 minutes. Strain through a fine sieve, discarding the shells. Wipe the pan clean.

3 Put the chillies, onion, garlic, ginger (or galangal), turmeric, ground coriander, lemongrass and 60 ml (2 fl oz/¼ cup) of the stock in a food processor and process until finely chopped.

4 Heat the remaining oil in the clean saucepan and add the chilli mixture and shrimp paste. Stir over low heat for 3 minutes, or until fragrant. Pour in the remaining stock and simmer for 10 minutes. Then add the coconut cream, palm sugar, makrut leaves and 2 teaspoons of salt. Simmer for a further 5 minutes.

5 Add the prawns and simmer for 2 minutes, until they are just pink. Remove and set aside. Add the fish balls and bean curd and simmer gently until just heated through.

6 Bring a pan of water to the boil and cook the noodles for 2 minutes, then drain and place in a bowl. Lay the bean sprouts and prawns on the noodles and pour the soup over the top. Sprinkle with the chopped mint and coriander leaves to serve.

Wearing rubber gloves, halve the chillies lengthways to remove the seeds.

Stir-fry the prawn shells, heads and tails until they turn bright orange.

Put the chillies, onion, garlic, lemongrass, spices and stock in a food processor.

Baby corn and chicken soup

PREPARATION TIME: 30 MINUTES | TOTAL COOKING TIME: 15 MINUTES | SERVES 4

150 g (5½ oz) whole baby corn (see NOTE)
1 tablespoon oil
2 lemongrass stems, white part only, very
    thinly sliced
2 tablespoons grated fresh ginger
6 spring onions (scallions), chopped
1 red chilli, finely chopped
1 litre (35 fl oz/4 cups) chicken stock
375 ml (13 fl oz/1½ cups) coconut milk
250 g (9 oz) boneless, skinless chicken breasts,
    thinly sliced
135 g (4¾ oz) creamed corn
1 tablespoon soy sauce
2 tablespoons finely snipped chives, to serve
1 red chilli, thinly sliced, to serve

1   Cut the baby corn in half or quarters
lengthways, depending on their size.

2   Heat the oil in a saucepan over medium heat
and cook the lemongrass, ginger, spring onion
and chilli for 1 minute, stirring continuously.
Add the stock and coconut milk and bring to the
boil—do not cover or the coconut milk
will curdle.

3   Add the corn, chicken and creamed corn
and simmer for 8 minutes, or until the corn
and chicken are just tender. Add the soy sauce,
season well and serve garnished with the chives
and chilli.

NOTE: *Tinned baby corn can be substituted for
fresh corn. Add during the last 2 minutes
of cooking.*

Grate the peeled fresh ginger on the fine side of
the grater.

Cut the baby corn lengthways into halves or
quarters, depending on its size.

NUTRITION PER SERVE
Protein 20 g; Fat 25 g; Carbohydrate 15 g; Dietary
Fibre 3 g; Cholesterol 30 mg; 1520 kJ (360 Cal)

Spicy lamb soup

PREPARATION TIME: 40 MINUTES | TOTAL COOKING TIME: 1 HOUR 30 MINUTES | SERVES 4–6

2 large onions, roughly chopped
3 red chillies, seeded and chopped
    (or 2 teaspoons dried chilli)
3–4 garlic cloves
2.5 cm (1 inch) piece fresh ginger, peeled and
    chopped
5 cm (2 inch) lemongrass, white part only,
    finely chopped
½ teaspoon ground cardamom
2 teaspoons ground cumin
½ teaspoon ground cinnamon
1 teaspoon ground turmeric
2 tablespoons peanut oil
1.5 kg (3 lb 5 oz) lamb neck chops
2–3 tablespoons vindaloo paste
600 ml (21 fl oz) coconut cream
3 tablespoons soft brown sugar
2–3 tablespoons lime juice
4 makrut (kaffir lime) leaves

1 Put the onion, chilli, garlic, ginger,
1 teaspoon ground black pepper, lemongrass,
cardamom, cumin, cinnamon and turmeric in a
food processor and process to a paste. Heat half
the oil in a large frying pan and brown the chops
in batches. Drain on paper towels.

2 Add the remaining oil to the pan and cook
the spice and vindaloo pastes for 2–3 minutes.
Add the chops and 1.75 litres (61 fl oz/7 cups)
water, cover and bring to the boil. Reduce the
heat and simmer, covered, for 1 hour. Remove
the chops from the pan and stir in the coconut
cream. Remove the meat from the bones, shred
and return to the pan.

3 Add the sugar, lime juice and makrut
leaves. Simmer, uncovered, over low heat for
20–25 minutes, until slightly thickened.

NUTRITION PER SERVE (6)
Protein 55 g; Fat 38 g; Carbohydrate 17 g; Dietary
Fibre 3 g; Cholesterol 166 mg; 2602 kJ (622 Cal)

Process the onion with the chilli, garlic and spices to make a paste.

Trim away any excess fat from the lamb chops before cooking.

Hot and sour lime soup with beef

PREPARATION TIME: 20 MINUTES I TOTAL COOKING TIME: 30 MINUTES I SERVES 4

1 litre (35 fl oz/4 cups) beef stock

2 lemongrass stems, white part only, halved

3 garlic cloves, halved

2.5 cm (1 inch) piece fresh ginger, sliced

3 very large handfuls coriander (cilantro), leaves and stalks separated

4 spring onions (scallions), thinly sliced

2 strips lime zest

2 star anise

3 small fresh red chillies, seeded and finely chopped

500 g (1 lb 2 oz) fillet steak, trimmed

2 tablespoons fish sauce

1 tablespoon grated palm sugar (jaggery)

2 tablespoons lime juice, or to taste

coriander (cilantro) leaves, to garnish

NUTRITION PER SERVE
Protein 31 g; Fat 7 g; Carbohydrate 7 g; Dietary Fibre 0.5 g; Cholesterol 84 mg; 900 kJ (215 Cal)

1 Put the stock, lemongrass, garlic, ginger, coriander stalks, half the spring onion, lime zest, star anise, 1 teaspoon chopped chilli and 1 litre (35 fl oz/4 cups) water in a saucepan. Bring to the boil and simmer, covered, for 25 minutes. Strain and return the liquid to the pan.

2 Heat a chargrill pan or barbecue flat plate until very hot. Brush lightly with olive oil and sear the steak on both sides until browned but very rare in the centre.

3 Reheat the soup, adding the fish sauce and palm sugar. Season with salt and black pepper. Add the lime juice to taste (you may want more than 2 tablespoons) to achieve a hot and sour flavour.

4 Add the remaining spring onion and the chopped coriander leaves to the soup. Slice the beef across the grain into thin strips. Curl the strips into a decorative pattern, then place in the centre of four deep wide serving bowls. Pour the soup over the beef and garnish with the remaining chilli and a few extra coriander leaves.

Bring the soup to the boil, then reduce the heat and simmer for 25 minutes.

Brown the fillet steak on a hot chargrill pan or plate, keeping it very rare in the centre.

Slice the beef along the grain and curl the strips into a decorative pattern.

Crab and corn soup

PREPARATION TIME: 15 MINUTES I TOTAL COOKING TIME: 10 MINUTES I SERVES 4

1½ tablespoons oil
6 garlic cloves, chopped
6 red Asian shallots (eschalots), chopped
2 lemongrass stems, white part only,
    finely chopped
1 tablespoon grated fresh ginger
1 litre (35 fl oz/4 cups) chicken stock
250 ml (9 fl oz/1 cup) coconut milk
375 g (13 oz/2½ cups) frozen corn kernels
2 x 170 g (6 oz) tins crabmeat, drained
2 tablespoons fish sauce
2 tablespoons lime juice
1 teaspoon shaved palm sugar (jaggery) or soft
    brown sugar

1   Heat the oil in a large saucepan, then add the garlic, shallots, lemongrass and ginger and cook, stirring, over medium heat for 2 minutes.

2   Pour the chicken stock and coconut milk into the saucepan and bring to the boil, stirring occasionally. Add the corn and cook for 5 minutes.

3   Add the crabmeat, fish sauce, lime juice and sugar and stir until the crab is heated through. Season to taste. Ladle into bowls and serve immediately.

NUTRITION PER SERVE
Protein 15 g; Fat 11 g; Carbohydrate 21.5 g; Dietary Fibre 3.5 g; Cholesterol 71.5 mg; 1016 kJ (240 Cal)

Peel off the outer layers of the Asian shallots before chopping.

Shave off thin slices of the palm sugar with a sharp knife.

When the soup comes to the boil, add the corn kernels and cook for 5 minutes.

Chicken noodle soup

PREPARATION TIME: 20 MINUTES + 10 MINUTES SOAKING | TOTAL COOKING TIME: 10 MINUTES | SERVES 4

3 dried Chinese mushrooms
185 g (6½ oz) dried thin egg noodles
1 tablespoon oil
4 spring onions (scallions), cut into fine shreds
1 tablespoon soy sauce
2 tablespoons rice wine, mirin or sherry
1.25 litres (44 fl oz/5 cups) chicken stock
½ small barbecued chicken, shredded
60 g (2¼ oz) sliced ham, cut into strips
90 g (3¼ oz/1 cup) bean sprouts
coriander (cilantro) leaves and thinly sliced
　　red chilli, to garnish

1 Soak the mushrooms in boiling water for 10 minutes to soften them. Squeeze dry, then remove the tough stems from the mushrooms and slice the caps thinly.

2 Cook the noodles in a large pan of boiling water for 3 minutes, or according to the packet directions. Drain and cut the noodles into shorter lengths with scissors.

3 Heat the oil in a large heavy-based saucepan. Add the mushrooms and spring onion. Cook for 1 minute, then add the soy sauce, rice wine and stock. Bring slowly to the boil and cook for 1 minute. Reduce the heat then add the noodles, shredded chicken, ham and bean sprouts. Heat through for 2 minutes without allowing to boil.

4 Use tongs to divide the noodles among four bowls, ladle in the remaining mixture, and garnish with coriander leaves and sliced chilli.

NOTE: *Rice wine and mirin are available at Asian food stores.*

VARIATION: *Udon noodles can be used instead of egg noodles.*

The easiest way to shred the meat from the barbecued chicken is with a fork.

Put the mushrooms in a bowl, cover with boiling water and leave to soak.

NUTRITION PER SERVE
Protein 25 g; Fat 10 g; Carbohydrate 35 g; Dietary Fibre 3 g; Cholesterol 80 mg; 1426 kJ (340 Cal)

Crab dumpling soup

PREPARATION TIME: 25 MINUTES | TOTAL COOKING TIME: 20 MINUTES | SERVES 4

170 g (6 oz) tin crabmeat, well drained

2 tablespoons finely chopped spring
    onions (scallions)

2 garlic cloves, finely chopped

2 teaspoons sesame oil

3 teaspoons chopped fresh ginger

12 small round gow gee (egg) or won ton
    wrappers

3 spring onions (scallions), extra

1.25 litres (44 fl oz/5 cups) chicken stock

1 tablespoon soy sauce

1 tablespoon mirin (see NOTE)

1 teaspoon sugar

NUTRITION PER SERVE
Protein 30 g; Fat 20 g; Carbohydrate 35 g; Dietary
Fibre 5 g; Cholesterol 50 mg; 1800 kJ (430 Cal)

1 To make the crab filling, mix the crab
with the chopped spring onion, half the garlic,
1 teaspoon of sesame oil and 1 teaspoon of
the ginger.

2 Place 2 teaspoons of the filling on one half
of each wrapper. Moisten the edge with some
water and fold over to form a crescent. Press
the edges together firmly. Lay the dumplings on
a lightly floured surface.

3 Cut the extra spring onions into thin
strips and set aside. Heat the remaining sesame
oil in a saucepan, add the remaining garlic and
ginger and cook over medium heat for
3–4 minutes, or until the garlic is lightly golden.
Add the stock, soy sauce, mirin and sugar.
Bring to the boil, add the spring onion strips
(reserving some to garnish) and simmer for
2–3 minutes.

4 Bring a large saucepan of water to the boil,
add 3–4 dumplings at a time and cook for
5 minutes, or until just cooked. Place in bowls,
ladle the stock over the dumplings, garnish with
the spring onion strips and serve.

NOTE: *Mirin is a Japanese sweetened rice wine
which is used frequently in cooking.*

Be sure to drain the crabmeat thoroughly so that
the filling is not too liquid.

Using a sharp knife, peel the ginger, cut into strips,
then chop finely.

Fold over the wrapper to enclose the filling and
press firmly.

Mulligatawny soup

PREPARATION TIME: 20 MINUTES | TOTAL COOKING TIME: 1 HOUR 15 MINUTES | SERVES 4

30 g (1 oz) butter
375 g (13 oz) chicken thigh cutlets, skin and
    fat removed
1 large onion, finely chopped
1 apple, peeled, cored and diced
1 tablespoon curry paste
2 tablespoons plain (all-purpose) flour
750 ml (26 fl oz/3 cups) chicken stock
3 tablespoons basmati rice
1 tablespoon chutney
1 tablespoon lemon juice
3 tablespoons pouring (whipping) cream

1 Heat the butter in a large heavy-based saucepan and brown the chicken for 5 minutes, then remove from the pan. Add the onion, apple and curry paste to the pan. Cook for 5 minutes, or until the onion is soft. Stir in the flour, cook for 2 minutes then add half the stock. Stir until the mixture boils and thickens.

2 Return the chicken to the pan with the remaining stock. Stir until boiling, reduce the heat, cover and simmer for 45 minutes. Add the rice and cook for a further 15 minutes.

3 Remove the chicken, dice the meat finely and return to the pan. Add the chutney, lemon juice, cream and salt and pepper to taste.

STORAGE: *Can be kept covered and refrigerated for up to 3 days.*

Once the mixture has thickened, return the browned chicken thighs to the pan.

Add the basmati rice to the soup for the last 15 minutes of cooking.

NUTRITION PER SERVE
Protein 25 g; Fat 16 g; Carbohydrate 25 g; Dietary
Fibre 2 g; Cholesterol 28 mg; 1396 kJ (333 Cal)

Soba noodle soup

PREPARATION TIME: 15 MINUTES + 5 MINUTES SOAKING | TOTAL COOKING TIME: 10 MINUTES | SERVES 4

250 g (9 oz) soba noodles
2 dried shiitake mushrooms
2 litres (70 fl oz/8 cups) vegetable stock
120 g (4¼ oz) snow peas (mangetouts), thinly
    sliced
2 small carrots, cut into thin strips
6 spring onions (scallions), cut into short
    lengths and thinly sliced lengthways
2 garlic cloves, finely chopped
2.5 cm (1 inch) piece fresh ginger, finely
    shredded
80 ml (2½ fl oz/⅓ cup) soy sauce
60 ml (2 fl oz/¼ cup) mirin or sake
90 g (3¼ oz/1 cup) bean sprouts

1   Cook the noodles according to the packet instructions and drain.

2   Soak the mushrooms in 125 ml (4 fl oz/ ½ cup) boiling water until soft. Drain, reserving the liquid. Remove the stalks and slice the mushroom caps.

3   Combine the vegetable stock, mushrooms, mushroom liquid, snow peas, carrot, spring onion, garlic and ginger in a large saucepan. Bring slowly to the boil, then reduce the heat to low and simmer for 5 minutes, or until the vegetables are tender. Add the soy sauce, mirin and bean sprouts. Cook for a further 3 minutes.

4   Divide the noodles among four large serving bowls. Ladle the hot liquid and vegetables over the top and serve immediately.

Cut the ginger into thin strips the size and shape of matchsticks.

Simmer the vegetables for 5 minutes, or until they are tender.

NUTRITION PER SERVE
Protein 13 g; Fat 1.5 g; Carbohydrate 30 g; Dietary Fibre 6 g; Cholesterol 11 mg; 1124 kJ (270 Cal)

Thai-style chicken and corn soup

PREPARATION TIME: 10 MINUTES | TOTAL COOKING TIME: 5 MINUTES | SERVES 4

2 litres (70 fl oz/8 cups) chicken stock

425 g (15 oz) tin corn kernels, undrained

8 spring onions (scallions), sliced

1 tablespoon finely chopped fresh ginger

4 small boneless, skinless chicken breasts, finely sliced

1 tablespoon sweet chilli sauce

1 tablespoon fish sauce

120 g (4¼ oz) rice vermicelli noodles

1 very large handful coriander (cilantro) leaves, chopped

2 teaspoons grated lime zest

2 tablespoons lime juice

1 Bring the chicken stock to the boil in a large saucepan over high heat. Add the corn kernels and liquid, spring onion and ginger, then reduce the heat and simmer for 1 minute.

2 Add the chicken, sweet chilli sauce and fish sauce and simmer for 3 minutes, or until the chicken is cooked through.

3 Meanwhile, place the noodles in a heatproof bowl and pour in enough boiling water to cover. Leave for 4 minutes, or until softened. Drain the noodles and cut them into shorter lengths.

4 Add the noodles, coriander, lime zest and lime juice to the soup and serve immediately.

NUTRITION PER SERVE
Protein 33 g; Fat 5 g; Carbohydrate 35 g; Dietary Fibre 5.8 g; Cholesterol 63 mg; 1327 kJ (317 Cal)

Add the corn kernels, spring onion and ginger to the chicken stock.

Place the noodles in a heatproof bowl and cover with boiling water.

Appetisers

Spring rolls

PREPARATION TIME: 40 MINUTES | TOTAL COOKING TIME: 25 MINUTES | MAKES 18

2 tablespoons oil
2 garlic cloves, chopped
2.5 cm (1 inch) piece fresh ginger, grated
100 g (3½ oz) lean minced (ground) pork
100 g (3½ oz) minced (ground) chicken
60 g (2¼ oz) raw minced (ground) prawns
  (shrimp)
2 celery stalks, finely sliced
1 small carrot, finely chopped
90 g (3¼ oz/½ cup) chopped water chestnuts
4 spring onions (scallions), chopped
75 g (2½ oz/1 cup) finely shredded cabbage
125 ml (4 fl oz/½ cup) chicken stock
4 tablespoons cornflour (cornstarch)
2 tablespoons oyster sauce
1 tablespoon soy sauce
2 teaspoons sesame oil
36 small square spring roll wrappers
oil, for deep-frying
sweet chilli sauce, for serving

1 Heat 1 tablespoon oil in a wok or frying pan and cook the garlic and ginger for 30 seconds. Add the minced pork, chicken and prawn and cook for 3 minutes, or until they are brown. Transfer to a bowl.

2 Wipe the pan, then heat the remaining tablespoon of oil and add the celery, carrot, water chestnuts, spring onion and cabbage. Stir over medium heat for 2 minutes. Combine the chicken stock, 1 tablespoon cornflour, oyster and soy sauces and salt and pepper, add to the vegetables and stir until thickened. Stir the sesame oil and vegetables into the meat mixture and cool. Mix the remaining cornflour with 80 ml (2½ fl oz/⅓ cup) water until smooth.

3 Place 1 spring roll wrapper on the work surface with a corner towards you. Brush all the edges with a little cornflour paste and cover with another wrapper. Brush the edges of the second wrapper and spread about 1½ tablespoons of the filling across the bottom corner of the wrapper. Fold the bottom corner up over the filling, fold in the sides and roll up firmly. Repeat with the remaining wrappers and filling. Heat the oil in a deep saucepan and fry the rolls, in batches, for 2–3 minutes, or until golden. Drain and serve with sweet chilli sauce.

NUTRITION PER SPRING ROLL
Protein 2 g; Fat 7 g; Carbohydrate 5 g; Dietary Fibre 1 g; Cholesterol 7 mg; 390 kJ (90 Cal)

Add the minced pork, chicken and prawn to the wok or frying pan and fry until brown.

Mix the stock, 1 tablespoon of cornflour, oyster and soy sauces and seasoning.

Fold the bottom corner over the filling and fold in the sides before rolling up.

Asian oysters

PREPARATION TIME: 15 MINUTES | TOTAL COOKING TIME: 5 MINUTES | SERVES 4

12 fresh oysters, on the shell
2 garlic cloves, finely chopped
2.5 cm (1 inch) piece fresh ginger, finely
    shredded
2 spring onions (scallions), finely sliced on
    the diagonal
60 ml (2 fl oz/¼ cup) Japanese soy sauce
60 ml (2 fl oz/¼ cup) peanut oil
coriander (cilantro) leaves, to garnish

1   Line a bamboo steamer with baking paper punched with holes. Arrange the oysters in the bamboo steamer. Place the garlic, ginger and spring onion in a bowl, mix together well and then sprinkle over the oysters. Spoon 1 teaspoon of soy sauce over each oyster, cover the steamer with a lid and place over a wok of simmering water. Make sure the water is not touching the steamer. Steam for 2 minutes.

2   Heat the peanut oil in a small saucepan until smoking and carefully drizzle a little over each oyster. Garnish with the coriander leaves and serve immediately.

Sprinkle the oysters with garlic, ginger and spring onion, then with soy sauce.

Heat the peanut oil until it is smoking, then drizzle over the oysters.

NUTRITION PER SERVE
Protein 3 g; Fat 15 g; Carbohydrate 1 g; Dietary
Fibre 0.5 g; Cholesterol 12 mg; 612 kJ (145 Cal)

Thai potato cakes

PREPARATION TIME: 20 MINUTES | TOTAL COOKING TIME: 25 MINUTES | SERVES 4

750 g (1 lb 10 oz) boiling potatoes, peeled
1–2 small red chillies, finely chopped
8 cm (3¼ inch) piece lemongrass, white part
    only, finely chopped
3 very large handfuls coriander (cilantro)
    leaves, chopped
8 spring onions (scallions), chopped
2 eggs, lightly beaten
3 tablespoons plain (all-purpose) flour
oil, for shallow-frying
sweet chilli sauce, for serving

1 Grate the potatoes, then squeeze dry in a tea
towel (dish towel) to remove as much moisture
as possible. Mix with the chilli, lemongrass,
coriander, spring onion, egg and flour.

2 Heat 1.5 cm (⅝ inch) of oil in a frying pan.
Use 2 heaped tablespoons of mixture to make
each cake and cook three or four cakes at a time,
for 3–4 minutes over medium heat. Turn and
cook for another 3 minutes, or until crisp and
cooked through. Drain on paper towels and
keep warm while cooking the remaining mixture.
Serve hot with sweet chilli sauce.

NUTRITION PER SERVE
Protein 9 g; Fat 15 g; Carbohydrate 30 g; Dietary
Fibre 4 g; Cholesterol 90 mg; 1340 kJ (320 Cal)

Coarsely grate the potatoes and then squeeze them as dry as you can.

Add the chilli, lemongrass, coriander, spring onion, egg and flour to the potato and mix through.

Turn the potato cakes over and cook until crisp and cooked through.

Satay chicken

PREPARATION TIME: 40 MINUTES + 30 MINUTES MARINATING | TOTAL COOKING TIME: 20 MINUTES | SERVES 4

500 g (1 lb 2 oz) boneless, skinless
    chicken thighs
1 onion, roughly chopped
2 lemongrass stems, white part only,
    thinly sliced
4 garlic cloves
2 red chillies, chopped
2 teaspoons ground coriander
1 teaspoon ground cumin
1 tablespoon soy sauce
60 ml (2 fl oz/¼ cup) oil, or as needed
1 tablespoon soft brown sugar
cucumber slices and chopped roasted
    peanuts, to garnish

PEANUT SAUCE
125 g (4½ oz/½ cup) crunchy peanut butter
250 ml (9 fl oz/1 cup) coconut milk
1–2 tablespoons sweet chilli sauce
1 tablespoon soy sauce
2 teaspoons lemon juice

1 Soak 20 wooden skewers in cold water for 30 minutes to prevent scorching. Cut the chicken into 20 thick flat strips and thread onto the skewers.

2 Mix the onion, lemongrass, garlic, chilli, coriander, cumin, ½ teaspoon of salt and soy sauce in a food processor until smooth, adding a little oil if necessary. Spread the mixture over the chicken, cover and refrigerate for 30 minutes.

3 To make the peanut sauce, stir all the ingredients and 125 ml (4 fl oz/½ cup) water over low heat, until the mixture boils. Remove from the heat. The sauce will thicken on standing.

4 Brush a very hot chargrill pan or barbecue flat plate with the remaining oil. Cook the skewers in batches for 2–3 minutes on each side, sprinkling with a little oil and brown sugar. Serve with the peanut sauce, cucumber slices and chopped peanuts, if desired.

NUTRITION PER SERVE
Protein 40 g; Fat 46 g; Carbohydrate 14 g; Dietary Fibre 5 g; Cholesterol 62 mg; 2590 kJ (620 Cal)

Thread one thick chicken strip onto each skewer, flattening it out on the skewer.

The peanut sauce will thicken when it is left to stand.

During cooking, sprinkle the chicken with oil and brown sugar to give it a good flavour and colour.

Won ton wrapped prawns

PREPARATION TIME: 20 MINUTES + 20 MINUTES REFRIGERATION | TOTAL COOKING TIME: 10 MINUTES | MAKES 24

24 raw prawns (shrimp)
1 teaspoon cornflour (cornstarch)
24 won ton wrappers
oil, for deep-frying
125 ml (4 fl oz/½ cup) sweet chilli sauce
1 tablespoon lime juice

1 Peel and devein the prawns, leaving the tails intact.

2 Mix the cornflour with 1 teaspoon water in a small bowl. Work with one won ton wrapper at a time, keeping the rest covered with a damp tea towel (dish towel) to prevent drying out. Fold a wrapper in half to form a triangle. Wrap a prawn in the wrapper, leaving the tail exposed. Seal at the end by brushing with a little of the cornflour mixture, then pressing gently. Spread the wrapped prawns on a baking tray, cover with plastic wrap and refrigerate for 20 minutes.

3 Fill a deep heavy-based saucepan one-third full of oil and heat to 180°C (350°F), or until a cube of bread dropped into the oil browns in 15 seconds. Cook the prawns in batches for 1½ minutes each batch, or until crisp, golden and cooked through. The cooking time may vary depending on the size of the prawns. Check the time by cooking one prawn and testing it before continuing. Remove the prawns from the oil with a slotted spoon and drain on crumpled paper towels.

4 Stir the sweet chilli sauce and lime juice together in a small bowl. Serve with the prawns.

Seal the wrapped prawns at the end with a dab of cornflour mix.

Remove the cooked prawns from the oil with a slotted spoon.

NUTRITION PER PRAWN
Protein 5 g; Fat 2 g; Carbohydrate 6 g; Dietary Fibre 0.5 g; Cholesterol 27 mg; 245 kJ (60 Cal)

Sesame chicken skewers

PREPARATION TIME: 10 MINUTES + AT LEAST 2 HOURS MARINATING | TOTAL COOKING TIME: 10 MINUTES | SERVES 4

60 ml (2 fl oz/¼ cup) oil
2 tablespoons soy sauce
2 tablespoons honey
1 tablespoon grated fresh ginger
1 tablespoon sesame oil
4 large boneless, skinless chicken breasts, cut
    into small cubes
8 spring onions (scallions), cut into
    short lengths
1 tablespoon sesame seeds, toasted (see HINT)

1 To make the marinade, whisk together the oil, soy sauce, honey, ginger and sesame oil. Thread the chicken and spring onion alternately onto 12 skewers and place in a glass dish. Pour the marinade over the skewers, cover and refrigerate for at least 2 hours or overnight.

2 Put the skewers on a grill (broiler) tray and place under a hot grill (broiler). Baste with the remaining marinade and cook, turning once, for 10 minutes, or until cooked through. Sprinkle with the sesame seeds to serve.

NOTE: *These kebabs can also be barbecued on a barbecue grill plate or flat plate.*

HINT: *To toast sesame seeds, place in a dry pan and shake over moderate heat until the seeds are golden.*

Thread the pieces of chicken and spring onion alternately onto the skewers.

Once the skewers are cooked, sprinkle with the toasted sesame seeds.

NUTRITION PER SERVE
Protein 55 g; Fat 25 g; Carbohydrate 13 g; Dietary Fibre 1 g; Cholesterol 120 mg; 2180 kJ (520 Cal)

Spicy potato and chickpea pancakes

PREPARATION TIME: 30 MINUTES + 30 MINUTES RESTING | TOTAL COOKING TIME: 20 MINUTES | SERVES 4

600 g (1 lb 5 oz) boiling potatoes
1 small onion
3 tablespoons chopped coriander (cilantro)
2 spring onions (scallions), finely sliced
4 tablespoons besan (chickpea flour)
2 teaspoons harissa (see NOTE)
pinch of cayenne pepper
1 egg, beaten
vegetable oil, for shallow-frying
1 teaspoon ground coriander
¼ teaspoon ground turmeric
¾ teaspoon cumin seeds

NUTRITION PER SERVE
Protein 10 g; Fat 15 g; Carbohydrate 30 g; Dietary
Fibre 6 g; Cholesterol 45 mg; 1315 kJ (315 Cal)

1 Grate the potatoes and onion, place in a bowl and cover with cold water.

2 Put the fresh coriander, spring onion, besan, harissa, ¾ teaspoon of salt, ¼ teaspoon of ground black pepper and cayenne pepper into another bowl. Mix together and stir in the egg. Heat 2 tablespoons of oil in a large non-stick frying pan and fry the ground coriander, turmeric and cumin seeds over medium–high heat, stirring, for 25–30 seconds. Add to the bowl.

3 Drain the potato and onion and wring out in a tea towel (dish towel) to dry. Add to the other ingredients and mix with your hands. Cover and set aside for 30 minutes. Wipe out the frying pan with paper towel and preheat the oven to very low 120°C (235°F/Gas ½).

4 Heat 1–2 tablespoons of the oil in the frying pan. Spoon a heaped tablespoon of potato mixture into the pan and flatten to a rough circle. Cook for 2–3 minutes on each side, or until golden. Keep warm while cooking the remaining mixture.

NOTE: *Harissa should be available from large supermarkets, otherwise try speciality shops.*

Grate the potato and onion and soak in cold water to remove the starch.

Use about a heaped tablespoonful of mixture to make each pancake.

Sesame tempura prawns

PREPARATION TIME: 15 MINUTES I TOTAL COOKING TIME: 10 MINUTES I SERVES 6

SOY DIPPING SAUCE
1 tablespoon grated fresh ginger
250 ml (9 fl oz/1 cup) Japanese soy sauce
1 tablespoon sesame seeds, toasted
1 tablespoon caster (superfine) sugar

oil, for deep-frying
125 g (4½ oz/1 cup) tempura flour
2 tablespoons sesame seeds
750 g (1 lb 10 oz) raw prawns (shrimp), peeled
    and deveined, tails left intact

1   Combine the soy dipping sauce ingredients in a small bowl.

2   Fill a deep, heavy-based saucepan one-third full of oil and heat to 180°C (350°F), or until a cube of bread dropped in the oil browns in 15 seconds. Place the tempura flour and the sesame seeds in a bowl and gradually stir in 185 ml (6 fl oz/¾ cup) iced water with chopsticks until just combined. (The batter should still be lumpy.)

3   Dip the prawns, 3–4 at a time, into the batter and deep-fry for 1–2 minutes, or until golden brown. Drain on crumpled paper towels and serve at once with the dipping sauce.

NUTRITION PER SERVE
Protein 32 g; Fat 4 g; Carbohydrate 30 g; Dietary
Fibre 2 g; Cholesterol 186 mg; 1203 kJ (287 Cal)

Mix together the ginger, soy sauce, sesame seeds and sugar to make a sauce.

Mix the tempura batter with chopsticks until it is just combined but still lumpy.

Deep-fry the prawns in small batches until they are golden brown.

Thai omelettes

PREPARATION TIME: 5 MINUTES I TOTAL COOKING TIME: 10 MINUTES I SERVES 4

2 tablespoons soy sauce
2 tablespoons kecap manis (see NOTE)
2 tablepoons dry sherry
4 tablespoons peanut oil
8 spring onions (scallions), sliced on
    the diagonal
1 tablespoon grated fresh ginger
500 g (1 lb 2 oz) button mushrooms, sliced
12 eggs
1 handful coriander (cilantro) leaves, chopped

1 Put the soy sauce, kecap manis and sherry in a small bowl and mix well. Heat half the peanut oil in a saucepan, add the spring onion and ginger, and cook over low heat for 3–4 minutes, or until the onion is soft but not brown. Add the soy sauce mixture and the mushrooms and stir over medium heat for 3 minutes, or until the mushrooms are soft. Keep warm.

2 Break 3 of the eggs into a bowl and lightly beat with 1 tablespoon water. Season with salt and pepper. Heat 1 teaspoon of the remaining peanut oil in a small non-stick frying pan, add the beaten eggs and cook over medium heat for 2–3 minutes, or until just set.

3 Spoon a quarter of the mushroom mixture onto one half of the omelette and top with a few chopped coriander leaves. Fold the omelette over and gently slide onto a warm plate. Top with a few more coriander leaves. Serve immediately for someone else to eat while you cook the remaining three omelettes.

NOTE: *Kecap manis is a thick, sweet soy sauce. If you can't find it, use regular soy sauce mixed with a little soft brown sugar.*

NUTRITION PER SERVE
Protein 24 g; Fat 35 g; Carbohydrate 4.5 g; Dietary Fibre 4 g; Cholesterol 540 mg; 1780 kJ (425 Cal)

Pour the beaten egg into a small frying pan and cook until lightly set.

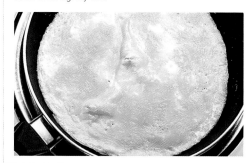

Add a quarter of the warm mushroom mixture to the omelette and top with some coriander leaves.

California rolls

PREPARATION TIME: 35 MINUTES + 15 MINUTES STANDING | TOTAL COOKING TIME: 15 MINUTES | MAKES 30

500 g (1 lb 2 oz/2¼ cups) short-grain white rice
60 ml (2 fl oz/¼ cup) rice vinegar
1 tablespoon caster (superfine) sugar
5 sheets nori (dried seaweed)
1 large Lebanese (short) cucumber, cut lengthways into long batons
1 avocado, thinly sliced
1 tablespoon black sesame seeds, toasted
30 g (1 oz) pickled ginger slices
125 g (4½ oz/½ cup) mayonnaise
3 teaspoons wasabi paste
2 teaspoons soy sauce

NUTRITION PER ROLL
Protein 1.5 g; Fat 3 g; Carbohydrate 15 g; Dietary Fibre 1 g; Cholesterol 1.5 mg; 380 kJ (90 Cal)

1 Wash the rice under cold running water, tossing, until the water runs clear. Put the rice and 750 ml (26 fl oz/3 cups) water in a saucepan. Bring to the boil over low heat and cook for 5 minutes, or until tunnels form in the rice. Remove from the heat, cover and leave for 15 minutes.

2 Place the vinegar, sugar and 1 teaspoon salt in a small saucepan and stir over low heat until the sugar and salt dissolve.

3 Transfer the rice to a non-metallic bowl and use a wooden spoon to separate the grains. Make a slight well in the centre, slowly stir in the vinegar dressing, then cool a little.

4 Lay a nori sheet, shiny side down, on a bamboo mat or flat surface and spread out one-fifth of the rice, leaving a clear border at one end. Arrange one-fifth of the cucumber, avocado, sesame seeds and ginger lengthways over the rice, to within 2.5 cm (1 inch) of the border. Spread with some of the combined mayonnaise, wasabi and soy sauce and roll to cover the filling. Continue rolling tightly to join the edges, then hold in place for a few seconds. Trim the ends and cut into slices. Serve with wasabi mayonnaise.

Cook the rice until tunnels appear, then cover and leave for 15 minutes.

Spread the wasabi mayonnaise mixture over the vegetables and start rolling.

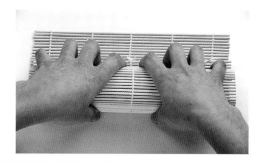
Roll the mat tightly to join the edges, then hold in place for a few seconds.

Salmon and prawn kebabs with Chinese spices

PREPARATION TIME: 15 MINUTES + AT LEAST 2 HOURS MARINATING | TOTAL COOKING TIME: 20 MINUTES | SERVES 6

4 x 200 g (7 oz) salmon fillets
36 raw prawns (shrimp), peeled, deveined,
 tails left intact
5 cm (2 inch) piece fresh ginger, finely
 shredded
170 ml (5½ fl oz/⅔ cup) Chinese rice wine
185 ml (6 fl oz/¾ cup) kecap manis
 (see NOTE, page 37)
½ teaspoon five-spice
200 g (7 oz) fresh egg noodles
600 g (1 lb 5 oz/1½ bunches) baby bok choy
 (pak choy)

1 Remove the skin and bones from the salmon
and cut into about 36 bite-sized cubes. Thread
three cubes of salmon alternately with three
prawns onto a skewer. Repeat with the remaining
ingredients to make 12 skewers. Lay the skewers
in a shallow non-metallic dish.

2 Mix together the ginger, rice wine, kecap
manis and five-spice. Pour over the skewers, then
cover and marinate for at least 2 hours. Turn the
skewers over a few times to ensure even coating.

3 Drain, reserving the marinade. Heat a
chargrill pan or barbecue flat plate and brush
with oil. Cook the skewers in batches for
4–5 minutes each side, or until cooked through.

4 Meanwhile, place the noodles in a bowl and
cover with boiling water. Leave for 5 minutes,
or until tender, then drain and keep warm. Place
the reserved marinade in a saucepan and bring to
the boil. Reduce the heat to a simmer. Separate
the bok choy leaves and add to the marinade,
stirring to coat. Cook, covered, for 1–2 minutes.

5 To serve, divide the noodles among six
serving plates. Top with the bok choy, then
the kebabs. Spoon on the marinade and
serve immediately.

Put the skewers in a shallow non-metallic dish and
pour over the marinade.

Cook the skewers on a chargrill pan or a barbecue
flat plate.

NUTRITION PER SERVE
Protein 50 g; Fat 15 g; Carbohydrate 24 g; Dietary
Fibre 5 g; Cholesterol 246 mg; 1856 kJ (440 Cal)

San choy bau

PREPARATION TIME: 20 MINUTES | TOTAL COOKING TIME: 10 MINUTES | SERVES 4

1 tablespoon peanut oil
1 teaspoon sesame oil
1–2 garlic cloves, crushed
1 tablespoon grated fresh ginger
4 spring onions (scallions), chopped
500 g (1 lb 2 oz) lean minced (ground) pork
1 red capsicum (pepper), seeded and diced
220 g (7¾ oz) tin water chestnuts, drained and
   roughly chopped
1–2 tablespoons soy sauce
1 tablespoon oyster sauce
2 tablespoons dry sherry
4 iceberg lettuce leaves

1 Heat the oils in a large, non-stick frying pan or wok. Add the garlic, ginger and spring onion and stir-fry for about 2 minutes. Add the minced pork and cook over medium heat until well browned, breaking up any lumps with a fork or wooden spoon.

2 Stir in the capsicum, water chestnuts, soy and oyster sauces and sherry. Simmer over medium heat until the liquid reduces and thickens. Keep warm.

3 Trim the edges of the lettuce leaves to make cup shapes and arrange on a plate. Spoon the pork filling into the lettuce leaves.

NUTRITION PER SERVE
Protein 32 g; Fat 13 g; Carbohydrate 25 g; Dietary Fibre 7 g; Cholesterol 60 mg; 1456 kJ (350 Cal)

Add the garlic, ginger and spring onion to the wok and stir for about 2 minutes.

Stir in the capsicum, water chestnuts, soy and oyster sauces and sherry.

Seekh kebabs

PREPARATION TIME: 40 MINUTES | TOTAL COOKING TIME: 12 MINUTES | SERVES 4

pinch of ground cloves
pinch of ground nutmeg
½ teaspoon chilli powder
1 teaspoon ground cumin
2 teaspoons ground coriander
3 garlic cloves, finely chopped
5 cm (2 inch) piece fresh ginger, grated
500 g (1 lb 2 oz) lean minced (ground) beef
1 tablespoon oil
2 tablespoons lemon juice

ONION AND MINT RELISH
1 red onion, finely chopped
1 tablespoon white vinegar
1 tablespoon lemon juice
1 tablespoon chopped fresh mint

NUTRITION PER SERVE
Protein 26 g; Fat 20 g; Carbohydrate 2 g; Dietary
Fibre 1 g; Cholesterol 80 mg; 1156 kJ (280 Cal)

1   Soak 12 thick wooden skewers in cold water for 30 minutes to prevent scorching. Dry-fry the cloves, nutmeg, chilli, cumin and coriander in a heavy-based frying pan, over low heat, for about 2 minutes, shaking the pan constantly. Transfer to a bowl with the garlic and ginger and set aside.

2   Knead the minced beef firmly using your fingertips and the base of your hand. The meat needs to be kneaded constantly for about 3 minutes, or until it becomes very soft and a little sticky. This process changes the texture of the meat when cooked, making it very soft and tender. Add the minced beef to the spice and garlic mixture and mix thoroughly, seasoning well.

3   Form tablespoons of the meat into small, round patty shapes. Wet your hands and press two portions of the meat around a skewer, leaving a gap of about 3 cm (1¼ inches) at the top of the skewer. Smooth the outside gently, place on baking paper and refrigerate while making the remaining kebabs.

4   To make the onion and mint relish, mix together the onion, vinegar and lemon juice and refrigerate for 10 minutes. Stir in the mint and season with pepper just before serving.

5   Grill the skewers or cook on an oiled barbecue grill plate or flat plate for about 8 minutes, turning regularly and sprinkling with a little lemon juice. Serve with the relish.

Finely chop the garlic and peel the fresh ginger and then grate.

Dry-fry the cloves, nutmeg, chilli, cumin and coriander in a heavy-based frying pan.

Press two rounds of meat around each wooden skewer, leaving space at the top of the skewer.

Vegetable tempura patties

PREPARATION TIME: 25 MINUTES | TOTAL COOKING TIME: 15 MINUTES | SERVES 4

WASABI MAYONNAISE
2 teaspoons wasabi paste
1 teaspoon Japanese soy sauce
125 g (4½ oz/½ cup) mayonnaise
1 teaspoon sake

½ carrot, cut into thin strips
½ onion, thinly sliced
100 g (3½ oz) orange sweet potato, grated
1 small zucchini (courgette), grated
1 small potato, cut into thin strips
4 spring onions (scallions), cut into
  matchsticks
4 sheets nori (dried seaweed), shredded
250 g (9 oz/2 cups) tempura flour, sifted
500 ml (17 fl oz/2 cups) chilled soda water
oil, for deep-frying
2 tablespoons shredded pickled ginger

1   To make the wasabi mayonnaise, stir together all the ingredients.

2   To make the patties, place the carrot, onion, orange sweet potato, zucchini, potato, spring onion and nori in a bowl. Toss together.

3   Place the tempura flour in a large bowl and make a well in the centre. Add the soda water and loosely mix together with chopsticks or a fork until just combined—the batter should still be lumpy. Add the vegetables and quickly fold through until just combined with the batter.

4   Fill a wok or deep heavy-based saucepan one-third full of oil and heat to 180°C (350°F). Gently drop a heaped tablespoon of the vegetable mixture into the oil and cook until golden. Drain on paper towels and season with sea salt. Repeat with the remaining mixture to make 12 patties. Serve immediately, topped with the wasabi mayonnaise and the pickled ginger.

Gently drop the vegetable patty mixture into the hot oil.

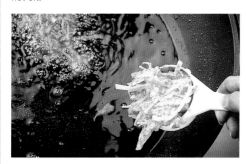

Deep-fry the patties until they are lightly brown and crisp.

NUTRITION PER SERVE
Protein 5.8 g; Fat 20 g; Carbohydrate 64 g; Dietary Fibre 3.5 g; Cholesterol 10 mg; 1948 kJ (465 Cal)

Tofu kebabs with miso pesto

PREPARATION TIME: 30 MINUTES + 1 HOUR MARINATING | TOTAL COOKING TIME: 10 MINUTES | SERVES 4

1 large red capsicum (pepper),
    cut into squares
12 button mushrooms, halved
6 baby onions, quartered
3 zucchini (courgettes), thickly sliced
450 g (1 lb) firm tofu, cut into small cubes
125 ml (4 fl oz/½ cup) olive oil
60 ml (2 fl oz/¼ cup) soy sauce
2 garlic cloves, crushed
2 teaspoons grated fresh ginger

MISO PESTO
90 g (3¼ oz) unsalted roasted peanuts
3 very large handfuls coriander (cilantro)
    leaves
2 tablespoons shiro miso (white miso)
2 garlic cloves
100 ml (3½ fl oz) olive oil

1   Soak 12 wooden skewers in cold water for 30 minutes to prevent scorching. Thread the vegetable pieces and tofu alternately onto the skewers, then place in a large shallow non-metallic dish.

2   Combine the olive oil, soy sauce, garlic and ginger, then pour half the mixture over the kebabs. Cover with plastic wrap and marinate for 1 hour.

3   To make the miso pesto, finely chop the peanuts, coriander leaves, miso paste and garlic in a food processor. Slowly add the olive oil while the machine is still running and blend to a smooth paste.

4   Heat a chargrill pan or barbecue flat plate and cook the kebabs, turning and brushing often with the remaining marinade, for 4–6 minutes, or until the edges are slightly brown. Serve with the miso pesto.

NUTRITION PER SERVE
Protein 8 g; Fat 64 g; Carbohydrate 10 g; Dietary Fibre 4 g; Cholesterol 0 mg; 2698 kJ (645 Cal)

Thread the vegetable pieces and tofu cubes alternately onto the skewers.

Mix the nuts, coriander leaves, miso and garlic until finely chopped.

Potato and coriander samosas

PREPARATION TIME: 1 HOUR | TOTAL COOKING TIME: 30 MINUTES | MAKES 24

50 g (1¾ oz) butter

2 teaspoons grated fresh ginger

2 teaspoons cumin seeds

1 teaspoon madras curry powder

½ teaspoon garam masala

500 g (1 lb 2 oz) boiling potatoes, peeled and finely diced

30 g (1 oz/¼ cup) sultanas (golden raisins)

90 g (3¼ oz/⅔ cup) frozen baby peas

1 very large handful coriander (cilantro) leaves

3 spring onions (scallions), sliced

1 egg, lightly beaten

oil, for deep-frying

thick plain yoghurt, to serve

SAMOSA PASTRY

450 g (1 lb) plain (all-purpose) flour, sifted

1 teaspoon baking powder

110 g (3¾ oz) butter, melted

125 g (4½ oz/½ cup) thick plain yoghurt

1   Heat the butter in a large non-stick frying pan, add the ginger, cumin seeds, curry powder and garam masala and fry lightly for 1 minute. Add the potato and 3 tablespoons water and cook over low heat for 15–20 minutes, or until the potato is tender. Toss the sultanas, peas, coriander and spring onion through the potato, remove from the heat and set aside to cool.

2   To make the samosa pastry, combine the flour, baking powder and 1½ teaspoons salt in a large bowl. Make a well in the centre and add the butter, yoghurt and 185 ml (6 fl oz/¾ cup) water. Using a flat-bladed knife, bring the dough together. Turn out onto a lightly floured surface and bring together to form a smooth ball. Divide the dough into four. Roll one piece out until it is very thin. Cover the remaining pastry until you are ready to use it.

3   Using a 12 cm (4½ inch) diameter bowl as a guide, cut out six circles. Place a tablespoon of potato filling in the centre of each circle, brush the edges of the pastry with egg and fold over to form a semi-circle. Make repeated folds on the rounded edge by folding a little piece of the pastry back as you move around the edge. Continue with the remaining pastry and filling.

4   Heat the oil in a deep heavy-based pan to 180°C (350°F). It is important not to have the oil too hot or the samosas will burn before the pastry has cooked. Add the samosas two or three at a time and cook until golden. Drain on paper towels. Serve with yoghurt.

NUTRITION PER SAMOSA
Protein 3 g; Fat 6 g; Carbohydrate 20 g; Dietary Fibre 1 g; Cholesterol 15 mg; 570 kJ (135 Cal)

Cut six circles from each sheet of pastry, using a bowl or plate as a guide.

Use a generous tablespoon of filling mixture for each samosa.

Make folds on the edge of the pastry, folding a piece back as you move around.

Chicken skewers with mango salsa

PREPARATION TIME: 20 MINUTES + AT LEAST 4 HOURS MARINATING | TOTAL COOKING TIME: 20 MINUTES | SERVES 4

4 boneless, skinless chicken thighs
1½ tablespoons soft brown sugar
1½ tablespoons lime juice
2 teaspoons green curry paste
18 makrut (kaffir lime) leaves
2 lemongrass stems

MANGO SALSA
1 small mango, finely diced
1 teaspoon grated lime zest
2 teaspoons lime juice
1 teaspoon soft brown sugar
½ teaspoon fish sauce

1 Cut the chicken thighs in half lengthways. Combine the brown sugar, lime juice, curry paste and two shredded makrut leaves in a bowl. Add the chicken and mix well. Cover and refrigerate for at least 4 hours.

2 Trim the lemongrass to measure about 20 cm (8 inches), leaving the root end intact. Cut each lengthways into four pieces. Cut a slit in each of the remaining makrut leaves and thread one onto each lemongrass skewer. Cut two slits in each piece of chicken and thread onto the lemongrass, followed by another makrut leaf. Repeat with the remaining makrut leaves, chicken and lemongrass. Pan-fry or barbecue until cooked through.

3 Gently stir together all the ingredients for the mango salsa and serve with the chicken skewers.

Cut each trimmed lemongrass stem lengthways into four pieces.

Thread a makrut leaf, then the chicken and another makrut leaf onto the lemongrass skewer.

NUTRITION PER SERVE
Protein 25 g; Fat 2.5 g; Carbohydrate 15 g; Dietary Fibre 1 g; Cholesterol 50 mg; 710 kJ (170 Cal)

Thai meatballs

PREPARATION TIME: 25 MINUTES | TOTAL COOKING TIME: 10 MINUTES | SERVES 4

350 g (12 oz) minced (ground) beef
3 French shallots (eschalots), finely chopped
3 garlic cloves, chopped
2.5 cm (1 inch) piece fresh ginger, grated
1 tablespoon green or pink
    peppercorns, crushed
2 teaspoons light soy sauce
2 teaspoons fish sauce
2 teaspoons soft brown sugar
1 very large handful coriander (cilantro) leaves
lime wedges
1 Lebanese (short) cucumber, chopped
3 sliced red or green chillies

1 Chop the minced beef with a cleaver or a large knife until very fine. Mix together the beef, shallots, garlic, ginger, peppercorns, light soy sauce, fish sauce and brown sugar.

2 Form 2 teaspoons of the mixture at a time into balls. Thread the balls onto eight wooden skewers, using three balls for each skewer.

3 Cook the skewers on an oiled hot chargrill pan or barbecue flat plate, turning frequently, for 7–8 minutes or until cooked through. Sprinkle with coriander. Serve with the lime wedges, cucumber and sliced chillies.

HINT: *Soak the wooden skewers in cold water for at least 30 minutes before use to prevent scorching.*

NUTRITION PER SERVE
Protein 20 g; Fat 10 g; Carbohydrate 3 g; Dietary Fibre 0 g; Cholesterol 55 mg; 700 kJ (170 Cal)

Use a large, sharp knife or a cleaver to chop the mince until very fine.

Form 2 teaspoons of mixture at a time into small compact balls.

Thai satay prawns

PREPARATION TIME: 30 MINUTES + AT LEAST 2 HOURS MARINATING | TOTAL COOKING TIME: 20 MINUTES | MAKES 6 SKEWERS

12 raw king prawns (shrimp)
1 garlic clove, crushed
80 g (2¾ oz/⅓ cup) smooth peanut butter
1 onion, grated
1 tablespoon fish sauce
½ teaspoon chilli flakes
1 teaspoon ground turmeric
5 coriander (cilantro) roots, finely chopped
170 ml (5½ fl oz/⅔ cup) coconut milk

SATAY SAUCE
2 teaspoons oil
1 teaspoon Thai red curry paste
1 lemongrass stem, white part only,
    finely chopped
2 teaspoons tamarind purée
250 ml (9 fl oz/1 cup) coconut milk
3 tablespoons smooth peanut butter
2 teaspoons sugar
2 teaspoons roasted unsalted peanuts,
    finely chopped

1 Soak six long wooden skewers in cold water for 30 minutes to prevent scorching. Peel and devein the prawns, leaving the tails intact.

2 Using a mortar and pestle or blender, make a marinade by blending the garlic, peanut butter, onion, fish sauce, chilli flakes, turmeric, coriander roots and about 2 tablespoons of the coconut milk until smooth. Stir in the remaining coconut milk.

3 Coat the prawns in the marinade, keeping the tails out if possible. Cover and refrigerate for at least 2 hours. Thread two prawns onto each skewer. Reserve the remaining marinade for the satay sauce, leaving a little to brush over the prawns during cooking.

4 To make the satay sauce, heat the oil in a small saucepan. Add the curry paste, lemongrass and tamarind and cook over high heat for 1 minute, or until aromatic. Add the coconut milk, peanut and sugar, bring to the boil, reduce the heat and simmer, uncovered, for 2 minutes. Stir in the reserved marinade and boil for 2 minutes, or until thickened.

5 Chargrill or barbecue the prawns until cooked through, turning once during cooking and brushing with the marinade. Serve immediately with the satay sauce, sprinkled with the chopped peanuts.

HINT: *The thickness of the sauce will depend on the peanut butter—if you prefer a more runny sauce, thin it with a little water.*

NUTRITION PER SKEWER
Protein 13 g; Fat 15 g; Carbohydrate 5 g; Dietary Fibre 1 g; Cholesterol 21 mg; 800 kJ (200 Cal)

Peel the prawns, leaving the tails intact, and then remove the veins.

Add the coconut milk, peanut butter and sugar to the pan and bring to the boil.

During the cooking, brush the prawns with the remaining marinade.

Miso yakitori chicken

PREPARATION TIME: 30 MINUTES | TOTAL COOKING TIME: 20 MINUTES | SERVES 4

1 kg (2 lb 4 oz) chicken thighs, skin on
3 tablespoons yellow or red miso paste
2 tablespoons sugar
60 ml (2 fl oz/¼ cup) sake
2 tablespoons mirin
1 Lebanese (short) cucumber
2 spring onions (scallions), cut into
    short lengths

1   Remove the bones from the chicken. Meanwhile, soak 12 wooden skewers in cold water for 30 minutes to prevent scorching. Place the miso, sugar, sake and mirin in a small saucepan over medium heat and cook, stirring well, for 2 minutes, or until the sauce is smooth.

2   Cut the chicken into bite-sized cubes. Seed the cucumber and cut into small batons. Thread the chicken, cucumber and spring onion alternately onto the skewers, using three pieces of each per skewer.

3   Cook on a chargrill pan or barbecue grill plate over high heat, turning occasionally, for 10 minutes, or until the chicken is almost cooked. Brush with the miso sauce and continue cooking, then turn and brush the other side. Repeat once or twice until the chicken and vegetables are cooked. Serve immediately.

NUTRITION PER SERVE
Protein 58 g; Fat 6.5 g; Carbohydrate 9 g; Dietary Fibre 0.5 g; Cholesterol 126 mg; 1377 kJ (329 Cal)

Remove the bones from the chicken thighs with a sharp knife.

Remove the seeds from the centre of the cucumber, then cut into batons.

Brush the chicken and vegetables with the miso sauce during cooking.

Salt-and-pepper squid

PREPARATION TIME: 30 MINUTES + 15 MINUTES MARINATING | TOTAL COOKING TIME: 10 MINUTES | SERVES 6

1 kg (2 lb 4 oz) squid tubes,
    halved lengthways
250 ml (9 fl oz/1 cup) lemon juice
125 g (4½ oz/1 cup) cornflour (cornstarch)
1 tablespoon ground white pepper
2 teaspoons caster (superfine) sugar
4 egg whites, lightly beaten
oil, for deep-frying
lemon wedges, to serve

1 Open out the squid tubes, wash and pat dry. Score a shallow diamond pattern on the inside, then cut into 5 x 3 cm (2 x 1¼ inch) pieces. Place in a flat non-metallic dish and pour on the lemon juice. Cover and refrigerate for 15 minutes. Drain well and pat dry.

2 Combine the cornflour, 1½ tablespoons of salt, white pepper and sugar in a bowl. Dip the squid into the egg white and lightly coat with the cornflour mixture, shaking off any excess.

3 Fill a deep heavy-based saucepan one-third full of oil and heat to 180°C (350°F), or until a cube of bread dropped into the oil turns golden brown in 15 seconds. Deep-fry the squid, in batches, for 1 minute each batch, or until the squid turns white and curls up. Drain on crumpled paper towels. Serve with the lemon wedges.

NUTRITION PER SERVE
Protein 31 g; Fat 9 g; Carbohydrate 22 g; Dietary Fibre 0.5 g; Cholesterol 332 mg; 1225 kJ (290 Cal)

Lightly score the squid with a diamond pattern and then cut into small rectangles.

Lightly coat the squid in the cornflour mixture, shaking off any access.

Thai fish cakes

PREPARATION TIME: 20 MINUTES | TOTAL COOKING TIME: 20 MINUTES | SERVES 6

500 g (1 lb 2 oz) red fish fillets, chopped
1 lemongrass stem, white part only, chopped
2 tablespoons fish sauce
5 spring onions (scallions), chopped
3 tablespoons chopped coriander (cilantro)
1 garlic clove, crushed
150 ml (5 fl oz) tin coconut milk
1 tablespoon sweet chilli sauce
1 egg
5 snake (yard long) beans, thinly sliced
oil, for shallow-frying

SAUCE
90 g (3¼ oz) sugar
2 tablespoons sweet chilli sauce
½ small Lebanese (short) cucumber, diced

1   Place the fish, lemongrass, fish sauce, spring onion, coriander, garlic, coconut milk, sweet chilli sauce and egg in a food processor and mix until smooth. Transfer to a bowl and fold in the snake beans. With wet hands, shape into twelve 8 cm (3¼ inch) cakes. Cover on a plate and refrigerate until ready to use.

2   For the sauce, stir the sugar and 80 ml (2½ fl oz/⅓ cup) water in a small saucepan over low heat for 2 minutes, or until all the sugar has dissolved. Increase the heat and simmer for 5 minutes, or until slightly thickened. Remove from the heat and stir in the sweet chilli sauce. Cool and stir in the diced cucumber.

3   Heat the oil in a large, deep, heavy-based frying pan and cook the fish cakes in batches over medium heat for 1–2 minutes on each side, or until cooked through. Serve with the sauce.

NUTRITION PER SERVE
Protein 21 g; Fat 11 g; Carbohydrate 19 g; Dietary Fibre 1.5 g; Cholesterol 89 mg; 1055 kJ (250 Cal)

Shape the mixture into 12 patties with wet hands to prevent sticking.

Remove the sugar syrup from the heat and stir in the sweet chilli sauce.

Cook the fish cakes on both sides, turning with a spatula, until cooked through.

Salads

Spiced lamb couscous salad

PREPARATION TIME: 25 MINUTES | TOTAL COOKING TIME: 35 MINUTES | SERVES 4–6

250 g (9 oz) lamb backstrap (tender eye of
   the lamb loin)
1 tablespoon mild curry powder
2 tablespoons pepitas (pumpkin seeds)
2 tablespoons sesame seeds
2 teaspoons cumin seeds
2 teaspoons coriander seeds
1 tablespoon oil
2 tablespoons lemon juice
1 onion, chopped
1 carrot, chopped
125 g (4½ oz) orange sweet potato, cubed
1 garlic clove, finely chopped

2 teaspoons oil, extra
185 g (6½ oz/1 cup) couscous
50 g (1¾ oz) raisins

NUTRITION PER SERVE (6)
Protein 15 g; Fat 10 g; Carbohydrate 30 g; Dietary
Fibre 3 g; Cholesterol 30 mg; 1135 kJ (270 Cal)

1 Sprinkle the lamb with the combined curry powder and a pinch of salt, then turn to coat well. Cover with plastic wrap and refrigerate while preparing the salad.

2 Place the pepitas and sesame seeds in a dry frying pan and cook, stirring, over medium–high heat until the seeds begin to brown. Add the cumin and coriander seeds and continue stirring until the pepitas begin to pop. Remove from the heat and allow to cool.

3 Heat the oil in a pan, add the lamb and cook over medium–high heat for 5–8 minutes, or until browned and tender. Remove from the pan, drizzle with half the lemon juice and leave to cool to room temperature. Turn the meat occasionally to coat in the lemon juice while cooling. To the same pan, add the onion, carrot and sweet potato and stir over high heat until the onion is translucent. Reduce the heat to medium, add 60 ml (2 fl oz/¼ cup) water, cover and cook for about 3 minutes. Stir in the chopped garlic and remaining lemon juice.

4 Pour 250 ml (9 fl oz/1 cup) boiling water into a heatproof bowl and add the extra oil. Add the couscous and stir until combined. Leave until the water has been absorbed. Fluff with a fork to separate the grains. Add the vegetable mixture, raisins and most of the toasted seeds, reserving some to sprinkle over the top, and toss. Spoon onto a serving plate. Slice the lamb and arrange over the salad. Drizzle with any left-over lemon juice and sprinkle with the reserved seeds.

Sprinkle the lamb backstrap with the combined curry powder and salt.

Fry the seeds in a dry frying pan until the pepitas puff up and begin to pop.

When the water has been absorbed, fluff the couscous with a fork.

Hokkien noodle salad

PREPARATION TIME: 20 MINUTES | TOTAL COOKING TIME: NIL | SERVES 8

900 g (2 lb) hokkien (egg) noodles
6 spring onions (scallions), sliced diagonally
1 large red capsicum (pepper), thinly sliced
200 g (7 oz/2 cups) snow peas (mangetouts),
    sliced
1 carrot, thinly sliced diagonally
3 very large handfuls mint, chopped
3 very large handfuls coriander (cilantro),
    chopped
100 g (3½ oz) roasted cashew nuts

SESAME DRESSING
2 teaspoons sesame oil
1 tablespoon peanut oil
2 tablespoons lime juice
2 tablespoons kecap manis (see NOTE,
    page 37)
3 tablespoons sweet chilli sauce

1 Gently separate the noodles and place in a
large bowl, cover with boiling water and leave for
2 minutes. Rinse and drain.

2 Put the noodles in a large bowl and add the
spring onion, capsicum, snow peas, carrot, mint
and coriander. Toss together well.

3 To make the dressing, whisk together the
oils, lime juice, kecap manis and sweet chilli
sauce. Pour the dressing over the salad and toss
again. Sprinkle the cashew nuts over the top and
serve immediately.

Top and tail the snow peas then finely slice
lengthways with a sharp knife.

Separate the noodles then put them in a large
bowl and cover with boiling water.

NUTRITION PER SERVE
Protein 10 g; Fat 9 g; Carbohydrate 35 g; Dietary
Fibre 4.5 g; Cholesterol 0 mg; 1115 kJ (265 Cal)

Vietnamese salad

PREPARATION TIME: 30 MINUTES + 10 MINUTES STANDING + 30 MINUTES REFRIGERATION | TOTAL COOKING TIME: NIL | SERVES 4–6

200 g (7 oz) dried rice vermicelli
140 g (5 oz/1 cup) crushed peanuts
1 large handful Vietnamese mint leaves, torn
1 very large handful coriander (cilantro) leaves
½ red onion, cut into thin wedges
1 green mango, cut into matchsticks
1 Lebanese (short) cucumber, halved
    lengthways and thinly sliced on
    the diagonal

LEMONGRASS DRESSING
125 ml (4 fl oz/½ cup) lime juice
1 tablespoon shaved palm sugar (jaggery)
60 ml (2 fl oz/¼ cup) seasoned rice vinegar
2 lemongrass stems, finely chopped
2 red chillies, seeded and finely chopped
3 makrut (kaffir lime) leaves, shredded

1   Place the rice vermicelli in a bowl and cover with boiling water. Leave for 10 minutes, or until soft, then drain, rinse under cold water and cut into short lengths.

2   Place the vermicelli, three-quarters of the peanuts, the mint, coriander, onion, mango and cucumber in a large bowl and toss together.

3   To make the dressing, place all the ingredients in a jar with a lid and shake together.

4   Toss the salad and dressing and refrigerate for 30 minutes. Sprinkle with the remaining nuts to serve.

Cut the green mango into short thin strips the size and shape of matchsticks.

Using scissors cut the rice vermicelli into shorter more manageable lengths.

NUTRITION PER SERVE (6)
Protein 6.5 g; Fat 13 g; Carbohydrate 19 g; Dietary Fibre 3 g; Cholesterol 0 mg; 926 kJ (221 Cal)

Sichuan chicken and noodle salad

PREPARATION TIME: 20 MINUTES | TOTAL COOKING TIME: 40 MINUTES | SERVES 4

5 cm (2 inch) piece fresh ginger, thinly sliced

5 spring onions (scallions)

2 chicken breasts, with bone and skin

1 teaspoon sichuan peppercorns (or whole
   black peppercorns)

250 g (9 oz) shanghai wheat noodles

1 teaspoon sesame oil

1 tablespoon light soy sauce

2 Lebanese (short) cucumbers, cut in half
   lengthways and thinly sliced

1½ tablespoons lime juice

1 very large handful coriander (cilantro)
   leaves

lime wedges, to serve

NUTRITION PER SERVE
Protein 28 g; Fat 5 g; Carbohydrate 34 g; Dietary
Fibre 2 g; Cholesterol 77 mg; 1255 kJ (300 Cal)

1   Bring a large saucepan of water to the boil. Add the ginger, 2 spring onions, thinly sliced, and 2 teaspoons salt and simmer for 10 minutes. Add the chicken and simmer gently for 15–20 minutes. Remove the chicken from the pan. When cool enough to handle, remove the skin and bones, then finely shred the flesh—there should be about 300 g (10½ oz) of shredded chicken. Place in a bowl and cover with plastic wrap. Refrigerate until ready to use.

2   Heat the peppercorns and 1 teaspoon salt in a small non-stick frying pan over medium–high heat. Dry-roast, stirring constantly, for 5 minutes, or until the salt begins to darken. Remove from the heat and cool. When cool, grind the salt and pepper mixture in a spice grinder or mortar and pestle, until very fine.

3   Cook the noodles in a saucepan of boiling water for 4–5 minutes, or until tender. Drain well and rinse under cold water. Place the noodles in a large bowl and toss with the sesame oil and soy sauce.

4   Sprinkle the salt and pepper mixture on the chicken and toss well, covering as much of the chicken as possible with the spice mixture. Thinly slice the remaining spring onions, then add to the chicken mixture with the cucumber and toss well. Add the chicken mixture and lime juice to the noodles and toss together. Top with the coriander and serve with lime wedges.

Remove the skin and bones from the chicken breasts and shred the flesh.

Toss the shanghai noodles, sesame oil and soy sauce in a large bowl.

Add the cucumber and spring onion to the seasoned chicken and toss well.

Tandoori lamb salad

PREPARATION TIME: 20 MINUTES + OVERNIGHT MARINATING | TOTAL COOKING TIME: 15 MINUTES | SERVES 4

250 g (9 oz/1 cup) low-fat plain yoghurt
2 garlic cloves, crushed
2 teaspoons grated fresh ginger
2 teaspoons ground turmeric
2 teaspoons garam masala
¼ teaspoon paprika
2 teaspoons ground coriander
red food colouring (optional)
500 g (1 lb 2 oz) lean lamb loin fillets
4 tablespoons lemon juice
1½ teaspoons chopped coriander (cilantro)
1 teaspoon chopped mint
150 g (5½ oz) mixed salad leaves
1 large mango, cut into strips
2 Lebanese (short) cucumbers, cut into
   matchsticks

1 Mix the yoghurt, garlic, ginger and spices in a bowl, add a little colouring and toss with the lamb to thoroughly coat. Cover and refrigerate overnight.

2 Grill the lamb on a foil-lined baking tray under high heat for 7 minutes each side, or until the marinade starts to brown. Set aside for 5 minutes before serving.

3 Mix the lemon juice, coriander and mint, then season. Toss with the salad leaves, mango and cucumber, then arrange on plates. Slice the lamb and serve over the salad.

Coat the lamb with the marinade, cover and refrigerate.

Cut the mango flesh into long thin strips using a sharp knife.

NUTRITION PER SERVE
Protein 30 g; Fat 6.5 g; Carbohydrate 8 g; Dietary Fibre 2 g; Cholesterol 90 mg; 965 kJ (230 Cal)

Chilli octopus salad

PREPARATION TIME: 15 MINUTES | TOTAL COOKING TIME: 5 MINUTES | SERVES 4

1.5 kg (3 lb 5 oz) baby octopus
250 ml (9 fl oz/1 cup) sweet chilli sauce
80 ml (2½ fl oz/⅓ cup) lime juice
80 ml (2½ fl oz/⅓ cup) fish sauce
60 g (2¼ oz/⅓ cup) soft brown sugar
oil, for chargrilling
200 g (7 oz) mixed salad leaves, to serve
lime wedges, to serve

1 Cut the head from the octopus and discard. With your index finger, push the hard beak up and out of the body. Discard. Rinse the octopus under cold water, drain and pat dry.

2 Mix together the sweet chilli sauce, lime juice, fish sauce and sugar.

3 Brush a chargrill plate or barbecue grill plate with oil and heat to very hot. Cook the octopus, turning, for 3–4 minutes, or until they change colour. Brush with a quarter of the sauce during cooking. Do not overcook. Serve immediately on a bed of salad greens with the remaining sauce and the lime wedges.

NUTRITION PER SERVE
Protein 43 g; Fat 11 g; Carbohydrate 25 g; Dietary Fibre 2.5 g; Cholesterol 500 mg; 1543 kJ (370 Cal)

Push the hard beak up and out of the body with your index finger.

Mix together the sweet chilli sauce, lime juice, fish sauce and sugar.

Cook the octopus, turning, until they change colour. Don't overcook or they'll become tough.

Thai beef salad

PREPARATION TIME: 35 MINUTES | TOTAL COOKING TIME: 10 MINUTES | SERVES 4

3 garlic cloves, finely chopped
4 coriander (cilantro) roots, finely chopped
3 tablespoons oil
400 g (14 oz) piece rump or sirloin steak
1 small soft-leaved lettuce, leaves separated
200 g (7 oz) cherry tomatoes, halved
1 Lebanese (short) cucumber, thickly sliced
4 spring onions (scallions), chopped
1 very large handful coriander (cilantro)
    leaves

DRESSING
2 tablespoons fish sauce
2 tablespoons lime juice
1 tablespoon soy sauce
2 teaspoons chopped red chillies
2 teaspoons soft brown sugar

1 Finely grind the chopped garlic, coriander roots, ½ teaspoon black pepper and 2 tablespoons of the oil in a mortar and pestle, food processor or blender. Spread evenly over the steak.

2 Heat the remaining oil in a heavy-based frying pan or wok over high heat. Add the steak to the pan and cook for about 4 minutes each side, turning once only during the cooking time. Remove and allow to cool.

3 Meanwhile, combine the lettuce, cherry tomatoes, cucumber and spring onion on a serving plate.

4 To make the dressing, stir together the fish sauce, lime juice, soy sauce, chillies and brown sugar until the sugar has dissolved.

5 Cut the steak into thin strips. Arrange over the salad and toss together very gently. Drizzle with the dressing and scatter the coriander over the top. Serve immediately.

HINT: *Be careful that you don't overcook the steak—it should be pink and, therefore, succulent and tender.*

NUTRITION PER SERVE
Protein 25 g; Fat 18 g; Carbohydrate 6 g; Dietary Fibre 0 g; Cholesterol 67 mg; 1160 kJ (280 Cal)

Grind the garlic, coriander roots, pepper and oil in a mortar and pestle, food processor or blender.

When the steak has cooled, use a sharp knife to cut it into thin strips.

Japanese scallop and ginger salad

PREPARATION TIME: 10 MINUTES I TOTAL COOKING TIME: 5 MINUTES I SERVES 4

300 g (10½ oz) fresh scallops, without roe
100 g (3½ oz) baby English spinach leaves
1 small red capsicum (pepper), very thinly
   sliced
50 g (1¾ oz) bean sprouts
30 ml (1 fl oz) sake
1 tablespoon lime juice
2 teaspoons shaved palm sugar (jaggery)
1 teaspoon fish sauce

1 Remove any veins, membrane or hard
white muscle from the scallops. Lightly brush
a chargrill pan or barbecue flat plate with oil.
Cook the scallops in batches on the chargrill
plate for 1 minute each side, or until just cooked.

2 Divide the spinach leaves, capsicum and bean
sprouts among four serving plates. Arrange the
scallops over the top.

3 To make the dressing, whisk together the
sake, lime juice, palm sugar and fish sauce. Pour
over the salad and serve immediately.

NOTE: *Sprinkle with toasted sesame seeds as
a garnish.*

NUTRITION PER SERVE
Protein 10 g; Fat 0.5 g; Carbohydrate 3.5 g; Dietary
Fibre 1.5 g; Cholesterol 25 mg; 274 kJ (65 Cal)

Remove any veins, membrane or hard white muscle
from the scallops.

Divide the spinach, capsicum and bean sprouts
among the plates.

Whisk together the sake, lime juice, palm sugar and
fish sauce.

Vietnamese chicken salad

PREPARATION TIME: 15 MINUTES | TOTAL COOKING TIME: 10 MINUTES | SERVES 4

3 boneless, skinless chicken breasts
1 red chilli, seeded and finely chopped
60 ml (2 fl oz/¼ cup) lime juice
2 tablespoons soft brown sugar
60 ml (2 fl oz/¼ cup) fish sauce
½ Chinese cabbage, shredded
2 carrots, grated
3 very large handfuls mint, shredded

1 Put the chicken in a saucepan, cover with water and bring to the boil, then reduce the heat and simmer for 10 minutes, or until cooked through.

2 While the chicken is cooking, mix together the chilli, lime juice, sugar and fish sauce. Remove the chicken from the water. Cool slightly, then shred into small pieces.

3 Combine the chicken, cabbage, carrot, mint and dressing. Toss well and serve immediately.

STORAGE: *Any leftovers can be used the next day in a stir-fry.*

NUTRITION PER SERVE
Protein 30 g; Fat 3 g; Carbohydrate 15 g; Dietary Fibre 3.5 g; Cholesterol 62 mg; 900 kJ (215 Cal)

Poach the chicken in water for 10 minutes, or until cooked through.

Mix together the chilli, lime juice, sugar and fish sauce.

Toss together the chicken, cabbage, carrot, mint and dressing.

Duck and Indian spiced rice salad

PREPARATION TIME: 20 MINUTES | TOTAL COOKING TIME: 1 HOUR | SERVES 4–6

DRESSING

80 ml (2½ fl oz/⅓ cup) oil

1 teaspoon walnut oil

1 teaspoon grated orange zest

1 tablespoon orange juice

1 tablespoon finely chopped preserved ginger

1 teaspoon sambal oelek (South-East Asian chilli paste)

1 teaspoon white wine vinegar

100 g (3½ oz) wild rice

oil, for cooking

50 g (1¾ oz/½ cup) pecans

½ teaspoon ground cumin

½ teaspoon garam masala

¼ teaspoon cayenne pepper

75 g (2½ oz) long-grain white rice

1 celery stalk, finely sliced

20 yellow pear tomatoes, cut in half lengthways

20 g (¾ oz) baby English spinach leaves

4 spring onions (scallions), thinly sliced

450 g (1 lb) Chinese barbecued duck, with skin, cut into pieces (see NOTE)

strips of orange zest, to garnish

1   To make the dressing, mix the ingredients together thoroughly. Season with salt and black pepper.

2   Rinse the wild rice under cold water and add to 300 ml (10½ fl oz) simmering water. Cook, covered, for 45 minutes, or until the grains puff open. Drain off any excess water.

3   Meanwhile, heat 2 teaspoons oil in a large frying pan. Add the pecans and cook, stirring, until golden. Remove from the pan and allow to cool. Coarsely chop the pecans. Add the cumin, garam masala, cayenne pepper and a pinch of salt to the pan, and cook for 1 minute, or until aromatic. Add the pecans and toss to coat.

4   Add the white rice to a pan of boiling water and simmer until tender. Drain and mix with the wild rice and pecans in a large, shallow bowl. Add the celery, tomato, spinach leaves and spring onion. Add half of the dressing and toss well. Arrange the pieces of duck on top with the skin uppermost. Drizzle with the remaining dressing and garnish with the orange zest.

NOTE: *Chinese barbecued duck can be purchased in any Chinatown, from many Asian stores or from your local Chinese restaurant.*

NUTRITION PER SERVE (6)
Protein 20 g; Fat 40 g; Carbohydrate 30 g; Dietary Fibre 6 g; Cholesterol 90 mg; 2325 kJ (555 Cal)

Finely slice the celery stalk, and halve the pear tomatoes lengthways.

Cook the wild rice, covered, until the grains puff open.

Return the chopped pecans to the pan and toss until well coated with the spices.

Thai prawn and noodle salad

PREPARATION TIME: 25 MINUTES | TOTAL COOKING TIME: 2 MINUTES | SERVES 4

DRESSING
2 tablespoons grated fresh ginger
2 tablespoons soy sauce
2 tablespoons sesame oil
80 ml (2½ fl oz/⅓ cup) red wine vinegar
1 tablespoon sweet chilli sauce
2 garlic cloves, crushed
80 ml (2½ fl oz/⅓ cup) kecap manis
   (see NOTE, page 37)

500 g (1 lb 2 oz) cooked large prawns (shrimp)
250 g (9 oz) dried instant egg noodles
5 spring onions (scallions), sliced diagonally
2 tablespoons chopped coriander (cilantro)
1 red capsicum (pepper), diced
100 g (3½ oz/1 cup) snow peas (mangetouts),
   sliced
lime wedges, to serve

1 For the dressing, whisk together the ginger, soy sauce, sesame oil, red wine vinegar, chilli sauce, garlic and kecap manis.

2 Peel and devein the prawns. Cut each prawn in half lengthways.

3 Cook the egg noodles in a large saucepan of boiling water for 2 minutes, or until tender, then drain thoroughly. Cool in a large bowl.

4 Add the dressing, prawns and remaining ingredients to the noodles and toss gently. Serve with the lime wedges.

Whisk all the dressing ingredients together in a large bowl.

Cut each of the peeled, deveined prawns in half lengthways with a very sharp knife.

NUTRITION PER SERVE
Protein 32 g; Fat 12 g; Carbohydrate 48 g; Dietary
Fibre 4 g; Cholesterol 176 mg; 1805 kJ (430 Cal)

Coconut prawn salad

PREPARATION TIME: 35 MINUTES + 30 MINUTES REFRIGERATION | TOTAL COOKING TIME: 30 MINUTES | SERVES 4

24 raw king prawns (shrimp), peeled and
    deveined, tails left intact
plain (all-purpose) flour, to coat
1 egg
1 tablespoon milk
60 g (2¼ oz/1 cup) shredded coconut
2 very large handfuls chopped coriander
    (cilantro) leaves, plus 1 tablespoon extra
2½ tablespoons oil
300 g (10½ oz) red Asian shallots (eschalots),
    chopped
2 garlic cloves, finely chopped
2 teaspoons grated fresh ginger
1 red chilli, seeds and membrane removed,
    thinly sliced
1 teaspoon ground turmeric
270 ml (9½ fl oz) coconut cream
2 makrut (kaffir lime) leaves, thinly sliced
2 teaspoons lime juice
2 teaspoons palm sugar (jaggery)
3 teaspoons fish sauce
oil, for shallow-frying
150 g (5½ oz) mixed lettuce leaves

1 Holding the prawns by their tails, coat in flour, then dip into the combined egg and milk and then into the combined coconut and coriander. Refrigerate for 30 minutes.

2 Heat the oil in a saucepan and cook the shallots, garlic, ginger, chilli and turmeric over medium heat for 3–5 minutes. Add the coconut cream, makrut leaves, lime juice, palm sugar and fish sauce. Bring to the boil, then reduce the heat and simmer for 2–3 minutes, or until thick.

3 Heat 2 cm (¾ inch) oil in a pan and cook the prawns in batches for 3–5 minutes, or until golden. Drain on paper towels and season. Add the coriander to the dressing. Toss the lettuce and prawns together and drizzle with the dressing.

NUTRITION PER SERVE
Protein 7.5 g; Fat 47 g; Carbohydrate 12 g; Dietary
Fibre 5 g; Cholesterol 55 mg; 2060 kJ (490 Cal)

Peel and devein the prawns, keeping the tails intact.

Dip the floured prawns into the egg, then in the coconut and coriander mixture.

Pork tenderloin and green mango salad

PREPARATION TIME: 45 MINUTES + 2–4 HOURS REFRIGERATION I TOTAL COOKING TIME: 10 MINUTES I SERVES 4

2 lemongrass stems, white part only,
    thinly sliced
1 garlic clove
2 red Asian shallots (eschalots)
1 tablespoon coarsely chopped fresh ginger
1 red bird's eye chilli, seeded
1 tablespoon fish sauce
1 very large handful coriander (cilantro)
1 teaspoon grated lime zest
1 tablespoon lime juice
2 tablespoons oil
2 pork tenderloins, trimmed

DRESSING
1 large red chilli, seeded and finely chopped
2 garlic cloves, finely chopped
3 coriander (cilantro) roots, finely chopped
1¼ tablespoons grated palm sugar (jaggery)
2 tablespoons fish sauce
60 ml (2 fl oz/¼ cup) lime juice

SALAD
2 green mangoes or 1 small green papaya,
    peeled, pitted and cut into matchsticks
1 carrot, grated
45 g (1½ oz/½ cup) bean sprouts
½ red onion, thinly sliced
3 tablespoons roughly chopped mint
3 tablespoons roughly chopped coriander
    (cilantro) leaves
3 tablespoons roughly chopped Vietnamese
    mint

1 Place the lemongrass, garlic, shallots, ginger, chilli, fish sauce, coriander, lime zest, lime juice and oil in a blender or food processor and process to a coarse paste. Transfer to a non-metallic dish. Coat the pork in the marinade, cover and refrigerate for between 2 and 4 hours.

2 Mix together all the ingredients for the salad dressing. Combine all the salad ingredients in a large bowl.

3 Preheat a chargrill pan or barbecue grill plate and cook the pork over medium heat for 4–5 minutes each side, or until cooked through. Remove from the heat, rest for 5 minutes, then slice.

4 With the salad as a bed, arrange the sliced pork in a circle in the centre of each plate and top with the dressing.

NUTRITION PER SERVE
Protein 60 g; Fat 14 g; Carbohydrate 20 g; Dietary Fibre 3 g; Cholesterol 122 mg; 1860 kJ (444 Cal)

Mix the marinade ingredients to a coarse paste in a food processor or blender.

Cook the pork on a chargrill pan or barbecue grill plate until cooked through.

Thai noodle salad

PREPARATION TIME: 25 MINUTES | TOTAL COOKING TIME: 5 MINUTES | SERVES 4

DRESSING
2 tablespoons grated fresh ginger
2 tablespoons soy sauce
2 tablespoons sesame oil
80 ml (2½ oz/⅓ cup) red wine vinegar
3–4 teaspoons sweet chilli sauce
2 garlic cloves, crushed
80 ml (2½ oz/⅓ cup) kecap manis (see NOTE, page 37)

250 g (9 oz) fine instant noodles
5 spring onions (scallions), sliced
2 tablespoons chopped coriander (cilantro)
1 red capsicum (pepper), chopped

100 g (3½ oz/1 cup) snow peas (mangetouts), sliced
500 g (1 lb 2 oz) cooked king prawns (shrimp), peeled, halved and deveined

1 To make the dressing, put the ingredients in a large bowl and whisk with a fork to combine.

2 Cook the noodles in a large pan of boiling water for 2 minutes and drain well. Add to the dressing and toss to combine. Leave to cool.

3 Add the remaining ingredients to the noodles and toss gently. Serve at room temperature.

Peel and finely grate the fresh ginger on the fine side of the grater.

Add the kecap manis to the other ingredients and mix to combine

NUTRITION PER SERVE
Protein 35 g; Fat 15 g; Carbohydrate 60 g; Dietary Fibre 3 g; Cholesterol 235 mg; 2275 kJ (540 Cal)

Spicy Indian lentil salad

PREPARATION TIME: 30 MINUTES | TOTAL COOKING TIME: 1 HOUR 10 MINUTES | SERVES 6

210 g (7½ oz) brown rice
185 g (6½ oz/1 cup) brown lentils
1 teaspoon turmeric
1 teaspoon ground cinnamon
6 cardamom pods
3 star anise
2 bay leaves
60 ml (2 fl oz/¼ cup) sunflower oil
1 tablespoon lemon juice
250 g (9 oz) broccoli florets
2 carrots, cut into matchsticks
1 onion, finely chopped
2 garlic cloves, crushed
1 red capsicum (pepper), finely chopped
1 teaspoon garam masala
1 teaspoon ground coriander
235 g (8½ oz/1½ cups) peas

MINT AND YOGHURT DRESSING

250 g (9 oz/1 cup) plain yoghurt
1 tablespoon lemon juice
1 tablespoon finely chopped mint
1 teaspoon cumin seeds

1 Put 750 ml (26 fl oz/3 cups) water with the rice, lentils, turmeric, cinnamon, cardamom, star anise and bay leaves in a pan. Stir to mix and bring to the boil. Reduce the heat, cover and simmer for 50–60 minutes. Remove the whole spices and discard. Transfer the mixture to a bowl. Whisk 2 tablespoons of the oil with the lemon juice and fork through the rice mixture.

2 Cook the broccoli and carrot until tender. Heat the remaining oil in a large saucepan and add the onion, garlic and capsicum. Stir-fry for 2–3 minutes, then add the garam masala and coriander. Cook 1–2 minutes. Add the vegetables and toss to coat. Add to the rice mixture and fork through to combine. Cover and refrigerate.

3 To make the dressing, mix all the ingredients, and season with salt and pepper. Serve the salad with the dressing.

Add the vegetables and toss to coat with the onion mixture.

NUTRITION PER SERVE
Protein 20 g; Fat 15 g; Carbohydrate 50 g; Dietary Fibre 10 g; Cholesterol 7 mg; 1605 kJ (380 Cal)

Miso tofu sticks with cucumber and wakame salad

PREPARATION TIME: 30 MINUTES + 20 MINUTES STANDING | TOTAL COOKING TIME: 15 MINUTES | SERVES 4

3 Lebanese (short) cucumbers, thinly sliced
20 g (¾ oz) dried wakame
500 g (1 lb 2 oz) silken firm tofu
3 tablespoons shiro miso
1 tablespoon mirin
1 tablespoon sugar
1 tablespoon rice vinegar
1 egg yolk
100 g (3½ oz) bean sprouts, blanched
2 tablespoons sesame seeds, toasted

DRESSING
3 tablespoons rice vinegar
¼ teaspoon soy sauce
1½ tablespoons sugar
1 tablespoon mirin

1   Sprinkle the cucumber generously with salt and leave for 20 minutes, or until very soft, then rinse and drain. To rehydrate the wakame, soak in plenty of water for 20–30 minutes, then drain well.

2   Place the tofu in a colander, weigh down with a plate and leave to drain.

3   Place the shiro miso, mirin, sugar, rice vinegar and 2 tablespoons water in a saucepan and stir over low heat for 1 minute, or until the sugar dissolves. Remove from the heat, then add the egg yolk and whisk until glossy. Cool slightly.

4   Cut the tofu into thick sticks and place on a non-stick baking tray. Brush the miso mixture over the tofu and cook under a hot grill (broiler) for 6 minutes each side, or until light golden on both sides.

5   To make the dressing, place all the ingredients and ½ teaspoon salt in a bowl and whisk together well.

6   To assemble, place the cucumber in the centre of a plate, top with the sprouts and wakame, drizzle with the dressing, top with the tofu and serve sprinkled with the sesame seeds.

NOTE: *Wakame is an edible seaweed. Shiro miso (white miso) is fermented paste of soy beans and usually either barley or rice. Both are available from Asian grocery stores and some supermarkets.*

NUTRITION PER SERVE
Protein 10 g; Fat 7 g; Carbohydrate 8 g; Dietary Fibre 2.5 g; Cholesterol 0 mg; 710 kJ (180 Cal)

Once the cucumber is very soft, rinse the salt off under running cold water.

Place the wakame in a colander and soak for 20–30 minutes in plenty of water.

Brush the miso mixture over the tofu sticks and grill (broil) until golden.

Tandoori chicken salad

PREPARATION TIME: 20 MINUTES + OVERNIGHT MARINATING | TOTAL COOKING TIME: 15 MINUTES | SERVES 4

4 boneless, skinless chicken breasts
2–3 tablespoons tandoori paste
200 g (7 oz) thick plain yoghurt
1 tablespoon lemon juice
1 very large handful coriander (cilantro) leaves
60 g (2¼ oz/½ cup) slivered almonds, toasted
snow pea (mangetout) sprouts, to serve

CUCUMBER AND YOGHURT DRESSING
1 Lebanese (short) cucumber, grated
200 g (7 oz) thick plain yoghurt
1 tablespoon chopped mint
2 teaspoons lemon juice

1 Cut the chicken breasts into thick strips. Combine the tandoori paste, yoghurt and lemon juice in a large bowl, add the chicken strips and toss to coat well. Refrigerate and leave to marinate overnight.

2 To make the dressing, put the grated cucumber in a medium bowl. Add the yoghurt, mint and lemon juice, and stir until well combined. Refrigerate until needed.

3 Heat a large non-stick frying pan, add the marinated chicken in batches and cook, turning frequently, until cooked through. Cool and place in a large bowl. Add the coriander leaves and toasted almonds, and toss until well combined. Serve on a bed of snow pea sprouts, with the dressing served separately.

NOTE: *The quality of the tandoori paste used will determine the flavour and look of the chicken. There are many good-quality varieties available from supermarkets and delicatessens.*

Combine the tandoori paste, yoghurt and lemon juice to make a marinade.

Using a metal grater, coarsely grate the Lebanese cucumber for the dressing.

NUTRITION PER SERVE
Protein 35 g; Fat 15 g; Carbohydrate 7 g; Dietary Fibre 2 g; Cholesterol 70 mg; 1230 kJ (290 Cal)

Japanese spinach salad

PREPARATION TIME: 25 MINUTES | TOTAL COOKING TIME: 5 MINUTES | SERVES 4

2 eggs
1 sheet nori (dried seaweed), cut into
    matchsticks
100 g (3½ oz) baby English spinach leaves
1 small red onion, finely sliced
½ small daikon radish, finely sliced
2 Lebanese (short) cucumbers, sliced
30 g (1 oz) pickled ginger, sliced
1 tablespoon toasted sesame seeds

DRESSING
80 ml (2½ fl oz/⅓ cup) light olive oil
1 tablespoon rice vinegar
1 tablespoon light soy sauce

1   Preheat the grill (broiler) to hot. Beat the
eggs lightly in a small bowl, add 1 tablespoon
water and the nori. Season well. Heat and
grease a 20 cm (8 inch) omelette pan. Pour in
the mixture to make a thin omelette. When
lightly browned underneath, place under the
grill (broiler) to set the top, without colouring.
Turn out onto a board and leave to cool. Cut the
omelette into thin strips.

2   To make the dressing, whisk together the
olive oil, vinegar and soy sauce until combined.
Toss together the spinach leaves, onion, daikon,
cucumber, ginger, sesame seeds, omelette strips
and dressing in a large bowl.

NUTRITION PER SERVE
Protein 5 g; Fat 25 g; Carbohydrate 15 g; Dietary
Fibre 2 g; Cholesterol 90 mg; 1235 kJ (295 Cal)

Peel the daikon radish and cut it into fine slices with a sharp knife.

Add 1 tablespoon water and the nori to the lightly beaten eggs.

Once the omelette has cooled, slice it into thin strips for adding to the salad.

Basmati rice, cashew and pea salad

PREPARATION TIME: 30 MINUTES + 30 MINUTES STANDING | TOTAL COOKING TIME: 20 MINUTES | SERVES 6

40 g (1½ oz) butter or ghee

½ teaspoon turmeric

300 g (10½ oz/1½ cups) basmati rice

200 g (7 oz) fresh or frozen peas, thawed

60 ml (2 fl oz/¼ cup) peanut oil

1 teaspoon yellow mustard seeds

1 teaspoon cumin seeds

30 g (1 oz/¼ cup) currants

1 garlic clove, crushed

1–2 small green chillies, finely chopped

1 teaspoon madras curry powder

100 ml (3½ fl oz) coconut cream

50 g (1¾ oz) glacé (candied) ginger, cut into thin strips

¼ small red onion, finely chopped

1 tablespoon chopped mint leaves

1 tablespoon chopped coriander (cilantro)

30 g (1 oz/½ cup) shredded coconut

100 g (3½ oz/⅔ cup) roasted cashew nuts, coarsely chopped

2 teaspoons shredded coconut, to garnish

NUTRITION PER SERVE
Protein 9 g; Fat 30 g; Carbohydrate 55 g; Dietary Fibre 6 g; Cholesterol 15 mg; 2110 kJ (500 Cal)

1   Melt the butter in a heavy-based saucepan and stir in the turmeric. Add the rice and ½ teaspoon salt, and stir for 10–15 seconds, then pour in 375 ml (13 fl oz/1½ cups) water. Stir over high heat until boiling, then reduce the heat until gently simmering. Simmer, covered with a tight-fitting lid, for 13 minutes without removing the lid. Remove the pan from the heat and leave, covered, for 10 minutes, then fluff gently with a fork. Add the peas, transfer to a large bowl and allow to cool.

2   Heat 2 teaspoons of the oil in a saucepan and stir in the mustard and cumin seeds. When the mustard seeds start to pop, add the currants, garlic, chilli and curry powder. Stir to combine, but do not brown. Stir in the coconut cream, remove from the heat and transfer to the bowl of rice and peas.

3   Add the ginger, onion, herbs and the remaining oil to the rice and peas. Toss well, and set aside for at least 30 minutes. Just before serving, toss through the coconut and cashew nuts. Garnish with the shredded coconut.

NOTE: *Rice salads often improve if made in advance. This dish may be prepared up to 24 hours in advance, but add the cashew nuts and shredded coconut just before serving to keep them crisp.*

Cut the glacé ginger into thin strips and chop the red onion and mint.

Add the rice and salt to the melted butter and turmeric in the saucepan.

Add the currants, garlic, chilli and curry powder to the mustard and cumin seeds.

Gado gado

PREPARATION TIME: 30 MINUTES | TOTAL COOKING TIME: 35 MINUTES | SERVES 4

6 new potatoes
2 carrots, cut into thick batons
250 g (9 oz) snake beans, cut into long lengths
2 tablespoons peanut oil
250 g (9 oz) firm tofu, cubed
100 g (3½ oz) baby English spinach leaves
2 Lebanese (short) cucumbers, cut into batons
1 large red capsicum (pepper), cut into batons
100 g (3½ oz) bean sprouts
5 hard-boiled eggs

PEANUT SAUCE
1 tablespoon peanut oil
1 onion, finely chopped
150 g (5½ oz/⅔ cup) peanut butter
60 ml (2 fl oz/¼ cup) kecap manis (see NOTE, page 37)
2 tablespoons ground coriander
2 teaspoons chilli sauce
185 ml (6 fl oz/¾ cup) coconut cream
1 teaspoon grated palm sugar (jaggery)
1 tablespoon lemon juice

1 Boil the potatoes until tender. Drain and cool slightly. Cut into quarters. Cook the carrot and beans separately in boiling water until just tender. Plunge into iced water, then drain.

2 Heat the oil in a non-stick frying pan and cook the tofu in batches. Drain on paper towels.

3 To make the peanut sauce, heat the oil in a frying pan over low heat and cook the onion for about 5 minutes. Add the peanut butter, kecap manis, coriander, chilli sauce and coconut cream. Bring to the boil, reduce the heat and simmer for 5 minutes. Stir in the palm sugar and juice until the sugar has dissolved. Arrange the vegetables and tofu on a plate. Halve the eggs and place in the centre. Serve with the sauce.

Using a sharp knife, cut the cucumbers and capsicum into even-sized batons.

Heat the oil and cook the tofu in batches until crisp and golden brown.

NUTRITION PER SERVE
Protein 35 g; Fat 55 g; Carbohydrate 35 g; Dietary Fibre 15 g; Cholesterol 265 mg; 3175 kJ (755 Cal)

Bok choy salad

PREPARATION TIME: 20 MINUTES | TOTAL COOKING TIME: 5 MINUTES | SERVES 4

250 ml (9 fl oz/1 cup) chicken stock
1 small carrot, cut into matchsticks
4 baby bok choy (pak choy)
100 g (3½ oz/1 cup) snow peas (mangetouts),
    thinly sliced
90 g (3¼ oz/1 cup) bean sprouts, trimmed
1 tablespoon chopped coriander (cilantro)

SESAME DRESSING
80 ml (2½ fl oz/⅓ cup) peanut oil
1 teaspoon sesame oil
1 tablespoon white vinegar
1 tablespoon sesame seeds, toasted (see HINT)
2 teaspoons grated fresh ginger
2 teaspoons honey, warmed
1 garlic clove, crushed

1   Pour the chicken stock into a frying pan and bring to the boil. Add the carrot and bok choy, cover and cook for 2 minutes. Drain the vegetables and leave to cool, then halve the bok choy lengthways.

2   To make the dressing, whisk together the oils, vinegar, sesame seeds, ginger, honey and garlic. Season with salt and pepper, to taste.

3   Place the cooled carrot strips and halved bok choy in a large serving dish and arrange the snow peas, bean sprouts and coriander on top. Drizzle with the sesame dressing.

HINT: *To toast the sesame seeds, place in a dry pan and shake gently over medium heat until the seeds smell fragrant and begin to turn a pale golden colour. Turn the seeds out onto a plate and leave to cool.*

NUTRITION PER SERVE
Protein 7 g; Fat 20 g; Carbohydrate 10 g; Dietary Fibre 4 g; Cholesterol 0 mg; 1110 kJ (265 Cal)

Cut the carrots into matchsticks for quick and even cooking.

Remove and discard the scraggly ends from the bean sprouts.

Noodles and rice

Phad thai

PREPARATION TIME: 25 MINUTES | TOTAL COOKING TIME: 10–15 MINUTES | SERVES 4

250 g (9 oz) thick rice-stick noodles

2 tablespoons oil

3 garlic cloves, chopped

2 teaspoons chopped red chillies

150 g (5½ oz) pork, thinly sliced

100 g (3½ oz) raw prawns (shrimp), peeled
    and chopped

½ bunch garlic chives, snipped

2 tablespoons fish sauce

2 tablespoons lime juice

2 teaspoons soft brown sugar

2 eggs, beaten

90 g (3¼ oz/1 cup) bean sprouts

sprigs of coriander (cilantro)

3 tablespoons chopped roasted peanuts, plus
    extra to serve (optional)

crisp fried onion and soft brown sugar,
    to serve (optional)

1   Soak the rice stick noodles in warm water for 10 minutes or until they are soft. Drain and set aside. Heat the oil to very hot in a wok or large frying pan, then add the garlic, chillies and pork and stir-fry for 2 minutes.

2   Add the prawn meat to the wok. Stir-fry for 3 minutes. Add the garlic chives and drained noodles to the wok, cover and cook for another minute.

3   Add the fish sauce, lime juice, sugar and eggs to the wok. Toss well until heated through.

4   To serve, sprinkle with bean sprouts, coriander and chopped peanuts. Traditionally served with crisp fried onion, soft brown sugar and more chopped peanuts on the side.

NUTRITION PER SERVE
Protein 20 g; Fat 10 g; Carbohydrate 10 g; Dietary
Fibre 2 g; Cholesterol 140 mg; 890 kJ (210 Cal)

After stir-frying the pork for 2 minutes, stir in the prawn meat.

Toss the ingredients using tongs or two wooden spoons, until heated through.

Sweet chilli chicken noodles

PREPARATION TIME: 10 MINUTES | TOTAL COOKING TIME: 10 MINUTES | SERVES 4–6

375 g (12 oz) hokkien (egg) noodles
4 boneless, skinless chicken thighs, cut into
  small pieces
1–2 tablespoons sweet chilli sauce
2 teaspoons fish sauce
1 tablespoon oil
100 g (3½ oz) baby sweet corn, halved
  lengthways
150 g (5½ oz) sugar snap peas, topped
  and tailed
1 tablespoon lime juice

1 Place the noodles in a large bowl, cover with boiling water and gently break apart with a fork. Leave for 5 minutes, then drain.

2 Combine the chicken, sweet chilli sauce and fish sauce in a bowl.

3 Heat a wok or frying pan over high heat, add the oil and swirl to coat. Add the chicken pieces and stir-fry for 3–5 minutes, or until cooked through. Then add the corn and sugar snap peas and stir-fry for 2 minutes. Add the noodles and lime juice and serve.

NUTRITION PER SERVE (6)
Protein 30 g; Fat 6.5 g; Carbohydrate 50 g; Dietary Fibre 4 g; Cholesterol 53 mg; 1593 kJ (380 Cal)

Cover the noodles with boiling water and gently break apart with a fork.

Put the chicken in a bowl with the sweet chilli and fish sauces.

Stir-fry the chicken until cooked through before adding the other ingredients.

Noodles with fried tofu

PREPARATION TIME: 10 MINUTES | TOTAL COOKING TIME: 5 MINUTES | SERVES 4

100 g (3½ oz) deep-fried tofu puffs
    (see NOTE)
2 tablespoons oil
1 onion, sliced
1 red capsicum (pepper), cut into squares
3 garlic cloves, crushed
2 teaspoons grated fresh ginger
120 g (4¼ oz/¾ cup) small chunks
    fresh pineapple
500 g (1 lb 2 oz) thin hokkien (egg) noodles,
    separated
60 ml (2 fl oz/¼ cup) pineapple juice
60 ml (2 fl oz/¼ cup) hoisin sauce
1 very large handful roughly chopped
    coriander (cilantro)

1   Slice the tofu puffs into three, then cut each slice into two or three pieces.

2   Heat the wok until very hot, add the oil and stir-fry the onion and capsicum for 1–2 minutes, or until beginning to soften. Add the garlic and ginger, stir-fry for 1 minute, then add the tofu and stir-fry for 2 minutes.

3   Add the pineapple chunks and noodles and toss until the mixture is combined and heated through. Add the pineapple juice, hoisin sauce and coriander and toss to combine. Serve immediately.

NOTE: *Deep-fried tofu puffs are available from the refrigerated section in Asian grocery stores and some supermarkets. They have a very different texture to ordinary tofu.*

NUTRITION PER SERVE
Protein 10 g; Fat 15 g; Carbohydrate 65 g; Dietary Fibre 3.5 g; Cholesterol 0 mg; 1830 kJ (435 Cal)

Use your fingers to gently separate the hokkien noodles before cooking.

Slice the deep-fried tofu puffs into three, then cut into pieces.

Rice stick noodles with chicken and greens

PREPARATION TIME: 25 MINUTES | TOTAL COOKING TIME: 10 MINUTES | SERVES 4

6 small bunches baby bok choy (pak choy)
8 stems Chinese broccoli
150 g (5½ oz) dried rice stick noodles
2 tablespoons oil
375 g (13 oz) boneless, skinless chicken
    breasts, cut into thin strips
2–3 garlic cloves, crushed
5 cm (2 inch) piece fresh ginger, grated
6 spring onions (scallions), cut into
    short lengths
1 tablespoon sherry
90 g (3¼ oz/1 cup) bean sprouts

SAUCE
2 teaspoons cornflour (cornstarch)
2 tablespoons soy sauce
2 tablespoons oyster sauce
2 teaspoons soft brown sugar
1 teaspoon sesame oil

NUTRITION PER SERVE
Protein 30 g; Fat 15 g; Carbohydrate 50 g; Dietary
Fibre 4 g; Cholesterol 45 mg; 1855 kJ (445 Cal)

1 Remove any tough outer leaves from the bok choy and Chinese broccoli. Cut into 4 cm (1½ inch) pieces across the leaves, including the stems. Wash well, then drain and dry thoroughly.

2 Place the rice stick noodles in a large heatproof bowl and cover with boiling water. Soak for 5–8 minutes, or until softened. Rinse, then drain. Cut into short lengths using scissors.

3 Meanwhile, to make the sauce, combine the cornflour and soy sauce in a small bowl. Mix to a smooth paste, then stir in the oyster sauce, brown sugar, sesame oil and 125 ml (4 fl oz/ ½ cup) water.

4 Heat the wok until very hot, add the oil and swirl it around to coat the side. Stir-fry the chicken strips, garlic, ginger and spring onion in batches over high heat for 3–4 minutes, or until the chicken is cooked. Remove from the wok and set aside.

5 Add the chopped bok choy, Chinese broccoli and sherry to the wok, cover and steam for 2 minutes, or until the vegetables are wilted. Remove from the wok and set aside. Add the sauce to the wok and stir until the sauce is glossy and slightly thickened. Return the chicken, vegetables, noodles and bean sprouts to the wok and heat through. Serve at once.

NOTE: *Broccoli and English spinach may be used as the greens.*

Cut the bok choy and Chinese broccoli into pieces across the leaves.

Cut the soaked noodles into short lengths to make them more manageable.

Sesame tofu rice

PREPARATION TIME: 20 MINUTES + OVERNIGHT REFRIGERATION + 30 MINUTES MARINATING | TOTAL COOKING TIME: 10 MINUTES | SERVES 4

300 g (10½ oz) firm tofu
2 teaspoons sesame oil
2 tablespoons soy sauce
1 tablespoon sesame seeds
2 tablespoons oil
3 zucchini (courgettes), sliced
150 g (5½ oz) button mushrooms, halved
    or quartered
1 large red capsicum (pepper), cut into squares
2 garlic cloves, crushed
550 g (1 lb 4 oz/3 cups) cold cooked brown
    rice (see NOTE)
1–2 tablespoons soy sauce, extra

1 Drain the tofu and pat dry with paper towels. Cut into cubes, place in a glass or ceramic bowl and add the sesame oil and soy sauce. Stir well and put in the refrigerator to marinate for 30 minutes, stirring occasionally.

2 Heat the wok until very hot, add the sesame seeds and dry-fry until lightly golden. Tip onto a plate to cool.

3 Reheat the wok, add the oil and swirl it around to coat the side. Remove the tofu from the bowl with a slotted spoon and reserve the marinade. Stir-fry the tofu over high heat, turning occasionally, for about 3 minutes, or until browned. Remove from the wok and set aside.

4 Add the vegetables and garlic, and cook, stirring often, until they are just tender. Add the rice and tofu, and stir-fry until heated through.

5 Add the toasted sesame seeds, the reserved marinade and the extra soy sauce to taste. Toss to coat the tofu and vegetables. Serve immediately.

NOTE: *Rice should be refrigerated overnight before making fried rice to let the grains dry out and separate.*

Dry-fry the sesame seeds until they are lightly golden brown.

NUTRITION PER SERVE
Protein 15 g; Fat 20 g; Carbohydrate 50 g; Dietary Fibre 5.5 g; Cholesterol 0 mg; 1815 kJ (435 Cal)

Singapore noodles

PREPARATION TIME: 20 MINUTES | TOTAL COOKING TIME: 10 MINUTES | SERVES 4–6

150 g (5½ oz) dried rice vermicelli
oil, for cooking
250 g (9 oz) Chinese barbecued pork
   (char siu), cut into small pieces
250 g (9 oz) raw prawns (shrimp), peeled and
   cut into small pieces
2 tablespoons madras curry powder
2 garlic cloves, crushed
1 onion, thinly sliced
100 g (3½ oz) shiitake mushrooms,
   thinly sliced
100 g (3½ oz) green beans, thinly sliced on
   the diagonal
1 tablespoon soy sauce
4 spring onions (scallions), thinly sliced on
   the diagonal

1   Place the vermicelli in a large bowl, cover
with boiling water and soak for 5 minutes. Drain
well and spread out on a clean tea towel (dish
towel) to dry.

2   Heat the wok until very hot, add
1 tablespoon of the oil and swirl it around to
coat the side. Stir-fry the pork and the prawn
pieces in batches over high heat. Remove from
the wok.

3   Reheat the wok, add 2 tablespoons of the
oil and stir-fry the curry powder and garlic for
1–2 minutes, or until fragrant. Add the onion
and mushrooms, and stir-fry over medium heat
for 2–3 minutes, or until the onion and
mushrooms are soft.

4   Return the pork and prawns to the wok, add
the beans and 2 teaspoons water, and toss to
combine. Add the drained noodles, soy sauce
and spring onion. Toss well and serve.

NUTRITION PER SERVE (6)
Protein 10 g; Fat 7.5 g; Carbohydrate 25 g; Dietary
Fibre 3 g; Cholesterol 60 mg; 905 kJ (215 Cal)

Cut the Chinese barbecued pork into slices, then
into small pieces.

Cover the vermicelli with boiling water in a
heatproof bowl and leave to soak.

Nasi goreng

PREPARATION TIME: 25 MINUTES + OVERNIGHT REFRIGERATION | TOTAL COOKING TIME: 15 MINUTES | SERVES 4–6

5–8 long red chillies, seeded and chopped

2 teaspoons shrimp paste

8 garlic cloves, finely chopped

oil, for cooking

2 eggs, lightly beaten

350 g (12 oz) boneless, skinless chicken thighs, cut into thin strips

200 g (7 oz) raw prawns (shrimp), peeled and deveined

1.5 kg (3 lb 5 oz/8 cups) cold cooked rice (see NOTE)

80 ml (2½ fl oz/⅓ cup) kecap manis (see NOTE, page 37)

80 ml (2½ fl oz/⅓ cup) soy sauce

2 small Lebanese (short) cucumbers, finely chopped

1 large tomato, finely chopped

lime wedges, to serve

1 Mix the chilli, shrimp paste and garlic to a paste in a food processor.

2 Heat the wok until very hot, add 1 tablespoon of the oil and swirl it around to coat the side. Add the beaten eggs and push the egg up the side of the wok to form a large omelette. Cook for 1 minute over medium heat, or until the egg is set, then flip it over and cook the other side for 1 minute. Remove from the wok and cool before slicing into strips.

3 Reheat the wok, add 1 tablespoon of the oil and stir-fry the chicken and half the chilli paste over high heat until the chicken is just cooked. Remove the chicken from the wok.

4 Reheat the wok, add 1 tablespoon of the oil and stir-fry the prawns and the remaining chilli paste until cooked. Remove from the wok and set aside.

5 Reheat the wok, add 1 tablespoon of the oil and the rice, and toss over medium heat for 4–5 minutes to heat through. Add the kecap manis and soy sauce and toss constantly until all of the rice is coated in the sauces. Return the chicken and prawns to the wok, and toss to heat through. Season well. Transfer to a serving bowl and top with the omelette strips, cucumber and tomato. Serve with the lime wedges.

NOTE: *Rice should be refrigerated overnight before making fried rice to let the grains dry out and separate.*

NUTRITION PER SERVE (6)
Protein 30 g; Fat 10 g; Carbohydrate 70 g; Dietary Fibre 3.5 g; Cholesterol 140 mg; 2105 kJ (505 Cal)

Remove the seeds from the chillies and finely chop the flesh.

Slit the peeled prawns down the backs to remove the vein.

Process the chilli, shrimp paste and garlic until a paste forms.

Chilli noodles with nuts

PREPARATION TIME: 20 MINUTES I TOTAL COOKING TIME: 12 MINUTES I SERVES 4

1½ tablespoons oil
1 tablespoon sesame oil
2–3 small red chillies, finely chopped
1 large onion, cut into thin wedges
4 garlic cloves, cut into paper-thin slices
1 red capsicum (pepper), cut into strips
1 green capsicum (pepper), cut into strips
2 large carrots, cut into thick matchsticks
100 g (3½ oz) green beans
2 celery stalks, cut into matchsticks
2 teaspoons honey
500 g (1 lb 2 oz) hokkien (egg) noodles,
    gently separated
100 g (3½ oz) dry-roasted peanuts
100 g (3½ oz) honey-roasted cashew nuts
30 g (1 oz) snipped garlic chives, or 4 spring
    onions (scallions), chopped
sweet chilli sauce and sesame oil, to serve

1   Heat the wok over low heat, add the oils and swirl them around to coat the side. When the oil is warm, add the chilli and heat until very hot.

2   Add the onion and garlic and stir-fry for 1 minute, or until the onion just softens. Add the capsicum, carrot and beans and stir-fry for 1 minute. Add the celery, honey and 1 tablespoon water and season with salt and pepper. Toss well, then cover and cook for 1–2 minutes, or until the vegetables are brightly coloured and just tender.

3   Add the noodles and nuts and toss well. Cook, covered, for 1–2 minutes, or until the noodles are heated through. Stir in the garlic chives and serve, drizzled with the sweet chilli sauce and sesame oil.

Peel the cloves of garlic, then cut them into paper-thin slices.

Remove the seeds from the capsicum and cut the flesh into strips.

NUTRITION PER SERVE
Protein 20 g; Fat 45 g; Carbohydrate 75 g; Dietary Fibre 7 g; Cholesterol 0 mg; 3330 kJ (795 Cal)

Coriander noodles with tuna

PREPARATION TIME: **15** MINUTES I TOTAL COOKING TIME: **10** MINUTES I SERVES **4**

60 ml (2 fl oz/¼ cup) lime juice
2 tablespoons fish sauce
2 tablespoons sweet chilli sauce
2 teaspoons grated palm sugar (jaggery)
1 teaspoon sesame oil
1 garlic clove, finely chopped
1 tablespoon virgin olive oil
4 tuna steaks, at room temperature
200 g (7 oz) dried thin wheat noodles
6 spring onions (scallions), thinly sliced
2 very large handfuls coriander (cilantro)
    leaves, chopped, plus extra leaves, to
    garnish
lime wedges, to garnish

1   To make the dressing, mix together the lime juice, fish sauce, sweet chilli sauce, palm sugar, sesame oil and garlic.

2   Heat the olive oil in a chargrill pan. Add the tuna steaks and cook over high heat for 2 minutes each side, or until cooked to your liking. Transfer the steaks to a warm plate, cover and keep warm.

3   Place the noodles in a large saucepan of lightly salted, rapidly boiling water and return to the boil. Cook for 4 minutes, or until the noodles are tender. Drain well. Add half the dressing and half the spring onion and coriander to the noodles and gently toss together.

4   Either cut the tuna into even cubes or slice it. Arrange the noodles on plates and top with the tuna. Mix the remaining dressing with the spring onion and coriander and drizzle over the tuna. Garnish with lime wedges and coriander.

NOTE: *If you prefer, serve the tuna steaks whole. If serving whole, they would look better served with the noodles on the side.*

NUTRITION PER SERVE
Protein 32 g; Fat 10 g; Carbohydrate 5 g; Dietary
Fibre 1 g; Cholesterol 105 mg; 1030 kJ (245 Cal)

Cook the tuna steaks in a chargrill pan until cooked to your liking.

Cook the noodles in lightly salted water for 4 minutes, or until tender.

Noodle cakes with Chinese barbecued pork

PREPARATION TIME: 45 MINUTES | TOTAL COOKING TIME: 25 MINUTES | SERVES 4

500 g (1 lb 2 oz) thin fresh rice noodles, at room temperature
2 Lebanese (short) cucumbers, halved lengthways and thinly sliced
2 tablespoons chopped coriander (cilantro) leaves
1 tablespoon lime juice
1 tablespoon fish sauce
2 teaspoons caster (superfine) sugar
60 ml (2 fl oz/¼ cup) oil
1 red capsicum (pepper), thinly sliced
3 garlic cloves, finely chopped
1 tablespoon white vinegar
60 ml (2 fl oz/¼ cup) black bean sauce
80 ml (2¾ fl oz/⅓ cup) chicken stock
1 tablespoon soft brown sugar
300 g (10½ oz) Chinese barbecued pork (char siu), sliced

NUTRITION PER SERVE
Protein 34 g; Fat 28 g; Carbohydrate 100 g; Dietary Fibre 7 g; Cholesterol 70 mg; 3360 kJ (805 Cal)

1 Pour boiling water over the noodles and leave for 5 minutes, or until softened. Drain, then gently separate.

2 To make the cucumber salad, toss the cucumber, coriander, lime juice, fish sauce and caster sugar together in a large bowl and leave until needed.

3 Heat 1 tablespoon of the oil in a large non-stick frying pan. Place four 10 cm (4 inch) egg rings in the frying pan. Fill as firmly as possible with the noodles and press down with the back of a spoon. Cook over medium heat for 10 minutes, or until crisp, pressing the noodles down occasionally. Turn over and repeat on the other side, adding another tablespoon of the oil if necessary. Cover and keep warm.

4 Meanwhile, heat 1 tablespoon of the remaining oil in a wok, add the capsicum and stir-fry over high heat for 2 minutes, or until softened slightly. Add the garlic to the wok and toss for 1 minute, or until softened, then add the vinegar, black bean sauce, stock and brown sugar. Stir until the sugar has dissolved, then simmer for 2 minutes, or until the sauce thickens slightly. Add the pork and stir to coat with the sauce.

5 To serve, place a noodle cake on each plate and top with some of the pork. Arrange the salad around the noodle cake and serve.

Soak the noodles in boiling water until they are soft, then gently separate them.

Press the noodles down into rings with the back of a spoon.

Simmer until the sugar dissolves and the sauce slightly thickens.

Vegetarian phad thai

PREPARATION TIME: 20 MINUTES | TOTAL COOKING TIME: 15 MINUTES | SERVES 4

400 g (14 oz) flat rice-stick noodles
2 tablespoons peanut oil
2 eggs, lightly beaten
1 onion, cut into thin wedges
2 garlic cloves, crushed
1 small red capsicum (pepper), thinly sliced
100 g (3½ oz) fried tofu, cut into thin strips
6 spring onions (scallions), thinly sliced
2 very large handfuls coriander (cilantro)
    leaves, chopped
60 ml (2 fl oz/¼ cup) soy sauce
2 tablespoons lime juice
1 tablespoon soft brown sugar
2 teaspoons sambal oelek (South-East Asian
    chilli paste)
90 g (3¼ oz/1 cup) bean sprouts
3 tablespoons chopped roasted
    unsalted peanuts

1 Cook the noodles in a saucepan of boiling water for 5–10 minutes, or until tender. Drain and set aside.

2 Heat a wok over high heat and add enough peanut oil to coat the bottom and side. When smoking, add the egg and swirl to form a thin omelette. Cook for 30 seconds, or until just set. Roll up, remove and thinly slice.

3 Heat the remaining oil in the wok. Add the onion, garlic and capsicum and cook over high heat for 2–3 minutes, or until the onion softens. Add the noodles, tossing well. Stir in the omelette, tofu, spring onion and half the coriander.

4 Pour in the combined soy sauce, lime juice, sugar and sambal oelek, then toss to coat the noodles. Sprinkle with the bean sprouts and top with roasted peanuts and the remaining coriander. Serve immediately.

Buy fried tofu for this dish (rather than the silken variety) and cut into thin strips.

Cook the egg, swirling the wok, to make a thin omelette, then roll up and thinly slice.

NUTRITION PER SERVE
Protein 13 g; Fat 21 g; Carbohydrate 34 g; Dietary Fibre 5 g; Cholesterol 90 mg; 1565 kJ (375 Cal)

Udon noodles

PREPARATION TIME: 15 MINUTES | TOTAL COOKING TIME: 10 MINUTES | SERVES 4

500 g (1 lb 2 oz) fresh udon noodles
1 tablespoon oil
6 spring onions (scallions), cut into
    short lengths
3 garlic cloves, crushed
1 tablespoon grated fresh ginger
2 carrots, cut into short lengths
150 g (5½ oz) snow peas (mangetouts), cut in
    half on the diagonal
100 g (3½ oz) bean sprouts
500 g (1 lb 2 oz) choy sum, cut into
    short lengths
2 tablespoons Japanese soy sauce
2 tablespoons mirin
2 tablespoons kecap manis (see NOTE,
    page 37)
2 sheets roasted nori (dried seaweed), cut into
    thin strips, plus extra, to garnish

1 Bring a saucepan of water to the boil, add the noodles and cook for 5 minutes, or until tender and not clumped together. Drain and rinse under hot water.

2 Heat the oil in a wok until hot, then add the spring onion, garlic and ginger. Stir-fry over high heat for 1–2 minutes, or until soft. Add the carrot, snow peas and 1 tablespoon water, toss well, cover and cook for 1–2 minutes, or until the vegetables are just tender.

3 Add the noodles, bean sprouts, choy sum, soy sauce, mirin and kecap manis, then toss until the choy sum is wilted and coated with the sauce. Stir in the nori just before serving. Garnish with the extra nori.

NUTRITION PER SERVE
Protein 25 g; Fat 7.5 g; Carbohydrate 95 g; Dietary Fibre 13 g; Cholesterol 22 mg; 2330 kJ (557 Cal)

Cut the roasted nori sheets into very thin strips. Nori is available from Asian speciality shops.

Cook the udon noodles until they are tender and not clumped together.

Prawn and pea noodle baskets

PREPARATION TIME: 40 MINUTES | TOTAL COOKING TIME: 25 MINUTES | SERVES 4

oil, for deep-frying
200 g (7 oz) fresh egg noodles
700 g (1 lb 9 oz) raw prawns (shrimp), peeled and deveined
2 spring onions (scallions), chopped
1 garlic clove, crushed
½ teaspoon finely grated fresh ginger
½ teaspoon sesame oil
½ teaspoon fish sauce
100 g (3½ oz/⅔ cup) peas, cooked
3 tablespoons sliced water chestnuts
1 tablespoon mint
2 teaspoons snipped chives
80 g (2¾ oz) snow pea (mangetout) sprouts

1 Half-fill a deep-fryer or large saucepan with oil and heat to 180°C (350°F). Before the oil is too hot, dip in two wire baskets, one slightly smaller than the other, then shake dry. Drop a noodle into the oil: if the oil bubbles and the noodle turns golden in 8–10 seconds, the oil is hot enough.

2 Separate the noodles and divide into four bundles. Arrange the first batch inside the large basket and press the smaller basket inside to mould the noodles. Holding the handles firmly, ease the baskets into the oil, keeping the noodles under. Gently twist the top basket to help stop sticking, tipping from side to side, and cook the noodles to an even golden brown. Drain on paper towels. Repeat with the other noodles.

3 Heat 2 tablespoons of oil in a wok. Stir-fry the prawns, spring onion, garlic and ginger over high heat for 2 minutes, or until the prawns turn pink. Stir in the sesame oil, fish sauce, peas and water chestnuts. Remove from the heat, season and mix in the mint, chives and snow pea sprouts.

4 Pile the prawn and pea mixture into the noodle baskets and serve at once.

NUTRITION PER SERVE
Protein 40 g; Fat 15 g; Carbohydrate 15 g; Dietary Fibre 3 g; Cholesterol 260 mg; 1575 kJ (375 Cal)

Loosely separate the noodles and divide them into four bundles.

Arrange the first bundle of noodles inside the larger basket.

Fit the baskets together, hold firmly, then gently lower them into the oil.

Noodles with barbecued pork and greens

PREPARATION TIME: 20 MINUTES | TOTAL COOKING TIME: 25 MINUTES | SERVES 4

250 g (9 oz) fresh thick egg noodles
1 tablespoon oil
1 tablespoon sesame oil
250 g (9 oz) Chinese barbecued pork
    (char siu), cut into small cubes (see NOTE)
1 large onion, very thinly sliced
2 garlic cloves, finely chopped
400 g (14 oz) green vegetables (beans,
    broccoli, celery), cut into bite-sized pieces
2 tablespoons hoisin sauce
1 tablespoon kecap manis (see NOTE,
page 37)
100 g (3½ oz) snow peas (mangetouts)
3 baby bok choy (pak choy), leaves separated
230 g (8 oz) tin water chestnuts, sliced

1   Two-thirds fill a pan with water and bring to
the boil. Add the noodles and cook for about
3 minutes, or until just tender. Drain well.

2   Heat the wok until very hot, add the oils and
swirl them around to coat the side. Stir-fry the
pork over medium heat for 2 minutes, or until
crisp. Drain on paper towels.

3   Reheat the wok, add the onion and garlic and
stir-fry over very high heat for about 1 minute, or
until just softened. Add the vegetables and cook,
tossing regularly, for 2 minutes, or until just
softened. Stir in the hoisin sauce, kecap manis,
snow peas, bok choy, water chestnuts and
1 tablespoon of water. Cook for 2 minutes,
covered. Add the noodles and stir-fried pork,
and toss gently to combine. Serve immediately.

NOTE: *Chinese barbecued pork is also known as
char siu. You can buy it at Chinese barbecue shops.
You can use Asian greens instead of beans, broccoli
and celery.*

Cut the barbecued pork into strips, then into
small cubes.

Trim the base of the baby bok choy, then cut them
into quarters lengthways.

NUTRITION PER SERVE
Protein 10 g; Fat 20 g; Carbohydrate 60 g; Dietary
Fibre 10 g; Cholesterol 0 mg; 3910 kJ (930 Cal)

Curried chicken noodles

PREPARATION TIME: 20 MINUTES | TOTAL COOKING TIME: 10 MINUTES | SERVES 4

100 g (3½ oz) dried rice vermicelli
oil, for cooking
500 g (1 lb 2 oz) boneless, skinless chicken
    breasts, cut into thin strips
2 garlic cloves, crushed
1 teaspoon grated fresh ginger
2 teaspoons Asian-style curry powder
1 red onion, sliced
1 red capsicum (pepper), thinly sliced
2 carrots, cut into matchsticks
2 zucchini (courgettes), cut into matchsticks
1 tablespoon soy sauce

1   Place the vermicelli in a large bowl, cover with boiling water and soak for 5 minutes. Drain well and place on a tea towel (dish towel) to dry.

2   Heat the wok until very hot, add 1 tablespoon of the oil and swirl it around to coat the side. Stir-fry the chicken in batches over high heat until browned and tender. Remove all the chicken and drain on paper towels.

3   Reheat the wok, add 1 tablespoon of the oil and stir-fry the garlic, ginger, curry powder and onion for 1–2 minutes, or until fragrant. Add the capsicum, carrot and zucchini to the wok, and stir-fry until well coated in the spices. Add 1 tablespoon water and stir-fry for 1 minute.

4   Add the drained noodles and chicken to the wok. Add the soy sauce and toss well. Season with salt before serving.

Trim any excess fat from the chicken and cut the chicken into thin strips.

Cut the carrot into strips, the size and shape of matchsticks.

NUTRITION PER SERVE
Protein 30 g; Fat 15 g; Carbohydrate 25 g; Dietary Fibre 4 g; Cholesterol 60 mg; 1495 kJ (355 Cal)

Soba noodles with salmon and miso

PREPARATION TIME: 20 MINUTES | TOTAL COOKING TIME: 15 MINUTES | SERVES 6

300 g (10½ oz) soba noodles
1 tablespoon soya bean oil
3 teaspoons white miso paste
100 g (3½ oz) honey
1½ tablespoons sesame oil
6 salmon fillets, skin and bones removed
1 teaspoon chopped garlic
1 tablespoon grated fresh ginger
1 carrot, cut into matchsticks
6 small spring onions (scallions), thinly sliced
60 g (2¼ oz/1 cup) soya bean sprouts
80 ml (2½ fl oz/⅓ cup) rice vinegar
3 tablespoons light soy sauce
1 teaspoon sesame oil, extra
1 tablespoon sesame seeds, toasted
mustard cress, to serve

NUTRITION PER SERVE
Protein 8 g; Fat 9.5 g; Carbohydrate 56 g; Dietary
Fibre 2.5 g; Cholesterol 9 mg; 1423 kJ (340 Cal)

1 Preheat the oven to moderate 180°C (350°F/Gas 4). Fill a large saucepan three-quarters full with water and bring to the boil. Add the soba noodles and return to the boil. Cook for 1 minute, then add 250 ml (9 fl oz/ 1 cup) cold water. Boil for 1–2 minutes, then add another 250 ml (9 fl oz/1 cup) water. Boil for 2 minutes, or until tender, then drain and toss with ½ teaspoon of the soya bean oil.

2 Whisk together the miso, honey, sesame oil and 1 tablespoon water to form a paste. Brush over the salmon, then sear on a hot chargrill or frying pan for 30 seconds on each side. Brush the salmon with the remaining paste and place on a baking tray. Bake for 6 minutes, then cover and leave to rest in a warm place.

3 Heat the remaining soya bean oil in a wok. Add the garlic, ginger, carrot, spring onion and sprouts and stir-fry for 1 minute—the vegetables should not brown, but remain crisp and bright. Add the noodles, rice vinegar, soy sauce and extra sesame oil and stir-fry quickly to heat through.

4 Divide the noodles among six serving plates, top with a portion of salmon and sprinkle with the sesame seeds. Garnish with the mustard cress before serving.

Place the cooked soba noodles in a large bowl and toss with the soya bean oil.

Whisk together the miso, honey, sesame oil and water to make a paste.

Stir-fry the vegetables without browning until they are crisp and bright.

Chinese fried rice

PREPARATION TIME: 15 MINUTES + OVERNIGHT REFRIGERATION | TOTAL COOKING TIME: 10 MINUTES | SERVES 4

2 tablespoons peanut oil
2 eggs, lightly beaten and seasoned
2 teaspoons lard (optional)
1 onion, cut into wedges
250 g (9 oz) ham, cut into thin strips
750 g (1 lb 10 oz/4 cups) cold cooked rice
   (see NOTE)
3 tablespoons frozen peas
2 tablespoons soy sauce
4 spring onions (scallions), cut into
   short lengths
250 g (9 oz) cooked small prawns
   (shrimp), peeled

1   Heat 1 tablespoon of the peanut oil in a wok or large frying pan and add the eggs, pulling the set egg towards the centre and tilting the wok to let the unset egg run to the edge.

2   When it is almost set, break up the egg into large pieces to resemble scrambled eggs. Transfer to a plate.

3   Heat the remaining oil and lard in the wok, swirling to coat the base and side. Add the onion and stir-fry over high heat until clear and softened. Add the ham and stir-fry for 1 minute. Add the rice and peas and stir-fry for 3 minutes until the rice is heated through. Add the eggs, soy sauce, spring onion and prawns. Heat through and serve.

NOTE: *Rice should be refrigerated overnight before making fried rice to let the grains dry out and separate.*

VARIATION: *This dish is traditionally served as a snack or course in its own right rather than as an accompaniment to other dishes. You can include Chinese barbecued pork (char siu), Chinese sausage (lap cheong) or bacon instead of ham.*

Cut the ham into thin strips and the onion into wedges for cooking.

Once the egg is almost set, break it up into large pieces, a little like scrambled egg.

NUTRITION PER SERVE
Protein 32 g; Fat 20 g; Carbohydrate 56 g; Dietary Fibre 3 g; Cholesterol 222 mg; 2200 kJ (525 Cal)

Noodles with chicken and fresh black beans

PREPARATION TIME: 15 MINUTES | TOTAL COOKING TIME: 15 MINUTES | SERVES 2–3

2 teaspoons salted black beans
oil, for cooking
2 teaspoons sesame oil
500 g (1 lb 2 oz) boneless, skinless chicken
    thighs, thinly sliced
3 garlic cloves, very thinly sliced
4 spring onions (scallions), chopped
1 teaspoon sugar
1 red capsicum (pepper), sliced
100 g (3½ oz) green beans, cut into
    short pieces
300 g (10½ oz) hokkien (egg) noodles
2 tablespoons oyster sauce
1 tablespoon soy sauce
coriander (cilantro) leaves, to garnish

1 Rinse the black beans in running water.
Drain and roughly chop.

2 Heat the wok until very hot, add
1 tablespoon of oil and the sesame oil and swirl
it around to coat the side. Stir-fry the chicken in
three batches, until well browned, tossing
regularly. Remove from the wok and set aside.

3 Reheat the wok, add 1 tablespoon of the oil
and stir-fry the garlic and spring onion for
1 minute. Add the black beans, sugar, capsicum
and beans and cook for 1 minute. Sprinkle with
2 tablespoons of water, cover and steam for
2 minutes.

4 Gently separate the noodles and add to the
wok with the chicken, oyster sauce and soy
sauce, and toss well. Cook, covered, for about
2 minutes, or until the noodles are just softened.
Serve immediately, garnished with the coriander.

NUTRITION PER SERVE (3)
Protein 50 g; Fat 20 g; Carbohydrate 50 g; Dietary
Fibre 2 g; Cholesterol 85 mg; 2490 kJ (595 Cal)

Cut the chicken thighs into thin strips, removing
any excess fat.

Roughly chop the rinsed and drained salted
black beans.

Asian risotto cakes with scallops

PREPARATION TIME: 35 MINUTES + 3 HOURS 10 MINUTES REFRIGERATION | TOTAL COOKING TIME: 40 MINUTES | SERVES 4 AS A STARTER

500 ml (17 fl oz/2 cups) vegetable stock

2 tablespoons mirin

1 lemongrass stem, white part only, bruised

2 makrut (kaffir lime) leaves

3 coriander (cilantro) roots

2 tablespoons fish sauce

1 tablespoon butter

2–3 tablespoons peanut oil

3 red Asian shallots (eschalots), thinly sliced

4 spring onions (scallions), chopped

3 garlic cloves, chopped

2 tablespoons finely chopped fresh ginger

1½ teaspoons white pepper

150 g (5½ oz/⅔ cup) arborio rice

2 tablespoons toasted unsalted chopped peanuts

3 very large handfuls coriander (cilantro) leaves, chopped

2 garlic cloves, chopped, extra

1 teaspoon finely chopped fresh ginger, extra

60 ml (2 fl oz/¼ cup) lime juice

1–2 teaspoons grated palm sugar (jaggery)

vegetable oil, for pan-frying

plain (all-purpose) flour, to dust

1 tablespoon vegetable oil, extra

16 large white scallops without roe, beards removed

lime wedges, to serve

1   Heat the stock, mirin, lemongrass, makrut leaves, coriander, half the fish sauce and 250 ml (9 fl oz/1 cup) water in a saucepan and maintain at a low simmer. Heat the butter and 1 tablespoon of the peanut oil in a saucepan over medium heat until bubbling. Add the shallots, spring onion, garlic, ginger and 1 teaspoon of the white pepper and cook for 2–3 minutes. Stir in the rice and toss.

2   Add 125 ml (4 fl oz/½ cup) of the stock. Stir constantly over medium heat until nearly all the liquid is absorbed. Continue adding the stock ½ cup at a time, stirring constantly, for 20–25 minutes, or until all the stock is absorbed and the rice is tender. Remove from the heat, cool, then cover and refrigerate for 3 hours.

3   To make the pesto, finely chop the peanuts, coriander, extra garlic and ginger and the remaining pepper in a blender. With the motor running, add the lime juice, palm sugar and the remaining fish sauce and peanut oil and process until smooth. Divide the risotto into four balls. Mould into patties. Cover and refrigerate for 10 minutes. Heat the vegetable oil in a large frying pan over medium heat. Dust the patties with flour and cook in batches for 2 minutes each side. Drain on paper towels. Cover and keep warm.

4   Heat the extra vegetable oil in a clean frying pan over high heat. Cook the scallops in batches for 1 minute each side. Serve with the risotto cakes, pesto and lime wedges.

Cook the flour-dusted patties until they are crisp and golden.

NUTRITION PER SERVE
Protein 12 g; Fat 32 g; Carbohydrate 36 g; Dietary Fibre 2 g; Cholesterol 30 mg; 1987 kJ (475 Cal)

Kedgeree

PREPARATION TIME: 20 MINUTES I TOTAL COOKING TIME: 30 MINUTES I SERVES 4

600 g (1 lb 5 oz) smoked haddock
50 g (1¾ oz) butter
1 onion, finely chopped
2 teaspoons curry powder
1 teaspoon ground cumin
1 teaspoon ground coriander
2 teaspoons seeded and finely sliced
　　green chilli
200 g (7 oz/1 cup) basmati rice
660 ml (22¾ fl oz) chicken or
　　fish stock
1 cinnamon stick
80 ml (2½ fl oz/⅓ cup) pouring
　　(whipping) cream
2 hard-boiled eggs, finely chopped
2 tablespoons chopped parsley
2 tablespoons chopped coriander (cilantro)

1　Poach the haddock in a large shallow frying pan, skin side up: cover with boiling water and simmer very gently for about 10 minutes. The fish is cooked when the flesh can be flaked easily with a fork. Drain and pat dry with paper towels. Remove the skin and flake into bite-size chunks.

2　Heat the butter in a large saucepan and add the onion. Cook until golden, then add the curry powder, cumin, coriander and chilli. Cook, stirring, for 1 minute. Add the rice, stir well, then pour in the stock and add the cinnamon stick. Cover tightly and simmer over gentle heat for about 12 minutes, or until the rice is tender.

3　Remove the cinnamon stick and gently stir in the haddock. Fold through the cream, chopped egg and the herbs. Season and serve immediately.

When the fish is cooked, the flesh will flake easily when tested with a fork.

Add the rice to the onion, curry powder, cumin, coriander and chilli and stir well.

NUTRITION PER SERVE
Protein 45 g; Fat 25 g; Carbohydrate 45 g; Dietary Fibre 2 g; Cholesterol 255 mg; 2355 kJ (560 Cal)

Fried rice with coriander and basil

PREPARATION TIME: 20 MINUTES + OVERNIGHT REFRIGERATION | TOTAL COOKING TIME: 20 MINUTES | SERVES 4

2 tablespoons oil
2.5 cm (1 inch) piece pork fat, chopped
4 garlic cloves, chopped
2 tablespoons grated fresh ginger
2 teaspoons chopped red chillies
2 boneless, skinless chicken thighs, diced
100 g (3½ oz) pork loin, diced
470 g (1 lb 1 oz/2⅓ cups) cold cooked jasmine
    rice (see NOTE)
1 tablespoon fish sauce
2 teaspoons light soy sauce
2 spring onions (scallions), chopped
1 very large handful Thai basil leaves,
    chopped
1 very large handful coriander (cilantro)
    leaves, chopped

1   Heat the oil to very hot in a wok. Stir-fry the pork fat, garlic, ginger and chilli for 2 minutes.

2   Add the diced chicken and pork to the wok and stir-fry for 3 minutes, or until the meat changes colour. Break up any lumps in the rice; add to the wok and toss well to warm through. Add the sauces and toss through with the spring onions and herbs.

NOTE: *Rice should be refrigerated overnight before making fried rice to let the grains dry out and separate.*

Cut the pork loin into small dice with a sharp knife. You can use any lean cut of pork.

Add the pork fat, garlic, ginger and chilli to the wok and stir with a wooden spoon.

NUTRITION PER SERVE
Protein 40 g; Fat 14 g; Carbohydrate 100 g; Dietary Fibre 3 g; Cholesterol 70 mg; 2900 kJ (690 Cal)

Wheat noodles with ginger chicken

PREPARATION TIME: 20 MINUTES + SOAKING | TOTAL COOKING TIME: 10 MINUTES | SERVES 4

4 dried Chinese mushrooms
2 teaspoons cornflour (cornstarch)
2 tablespoons soy sauce
2 tablespoons oyster sauce
1 tablespoon mirin or sweet sherry
200 g (7 oz) dried wheat noodles
1 teaspoon sesame oil
oil, for cooking
2–3 garlic cloves, crushed
8 cm (3¼ inch) piece fresh ginger, cut
    into matchsticks
375 g (13 oz) boneless, skinless chicken
    breasts, thinly sliced
1 red onion, cut into thin wedges
6 spring onions (scallions), cut into
    short lengths
185 g (6½ oz) small field mushrooms,
    thickly sliced
90 g (3¼ oz/1 cup) bean sprouts
1 very large handful mint, chopped

1   Place the dried mushrooms in a small bowl and cover with hot water. Leave to soak for 10 minutes, or until softened. Drain and squeeze dry, then discard the tough stems and chop the mushroom caps finely.

2   Combine the cornflour with 60 ml (2 fl oz/¼ cup) water and mix to a fine paste. Add the soy sauce, oyster sauce and mirin.

3   Cook the noodles in a large pan of boiling salted water for 1–2 minutes, or according to the manufacturer's instructions. Drain and set aside.

4   Heat the wok until very hot, add the sesame oil and 1 tablespoon of the oil, and swirl it around to coat the side. Stir-fry the garlic, ginger and chicken strips in batches over high heat for 2–3 minutes, or until the chicken is cooked through. Remove from the wok and set aside.

5   Reheat the wok, add 1 tablespoon of the oil and stir-fry the red onion and spring onion for 1–2 minutes, or until softened. Add the dried and field mushrooms, then stir-fry the mixture for 1–2 minutes, or until tender. Remove from the wok and set aside.

6   Add the soy sauce mixture to the wok and stir for 1–2 minutes, or until the sauce is heated and slightly thickened. Return the chicken and vegetables to the wok with the sprouts, noodles and chopped mint. Stir until the noodles are coated with the sauce. Serve at once.

NUTRITION PER SERVE
Protein 30 g; Fat 9 g; Carbohydrate 45 g; Dietary Fibre 6 g; Cholesterol 45 mg; 1650 kJ (395 Cal)

Cover the dried mushrooms with hot water and leave to soak.

Cook the noodles in a large pan of boiling salted water for a couple of minutes.

Stir-fries and pan-fries

Teriyaki pork with soya beans

PREPARATION TIME: 20 MINUTES + 2 HOURS REFRIGERATION + 10 MINUTES RESTING | TOTAL COOKING TIME: 30 MINUTES | SERVES 4

1½ tablespoons soy sauce

3 teaspoons grated fresh ginger

1 garlic clove, crushed

60 ml (2 fl oz/¼ cup) peanut oil

60 ml (2 fl oz/¼ cup) dry sherry

750 g (1 lb 10 oz) pork fillet

2 tablespoons honey

300 g (10½ oz/5 cups) frozen soya beans

4 baby bok choy (pak choy), sliced in half lengthways

3 teaspoons sesame oil

2 teaspoons finely chopped fresh ginger, extra

1 garlic clove, crushed, extra

sesame seeds, toasted, to garnish

1   Place the soy sauce, ginger, garlic and 2 tablespoons each of the peanut oil and sherry in a large shallow non-metallic dish and mix well. Add the pork and turn gently to coat well. Cover and refrigerate for 2 hours, turning the meat occasionally. Preheat the oven to 180°C (350°F/Gas 4).

2   Remove the pork and drain well, reserving the marinade. Pat the pork dry with paper towels. Heat the remaining peanut oil in a large frying pan and cook the pork over medium heat for 5–6 minutes, or until browned all over. Transfer to a baking tray and roast for 10–15 minutes. Cover with foil and rest for 10 minutes.

3   Put the reserved marinade, honey, the remaining sherry and 80 ml (2½ fl oz/⅓ cup) water in a small saucepan and bring to the boil. Reduce the heat and simmer for 3–4 minutes, or until reduced to a glaze. Keep the glaze hot.

4   Cook the soya beans in a large covered saucepan of lightly salted boiling water for 1 minute, then add the bok choy and cook for a further 2 minutes. Drain. Heat the sesame oil in the same saucepan, add the extra ginger and garlic and heat for 30 seconds. Return the soya beans and bok choy to the pan and toss gently.

5   Slice the pork and serve over the vegetables. Spoon the glaze over the pork, sprinkle with sesame seeds and serve immediately.

NUTRITION PER SERVE
Protein 48 g; Fat 25 g; Carbohydrate 6.5 g; Dietary Fibre 5 g; Cholesterol 86 mg; 1899 kJ (455 Cal)

Cook the pork fillets over medium heat until they are browned all over.

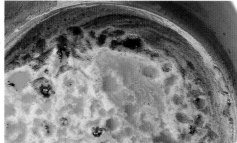
Simmer the marinade, honey and sherry mixture until reduced to a glaze.

Toss together the soya beans, bok choy, ginger and garlic.

Tempeh stir-fry

PREPARATION TIME: 15 MINUTES | TOTAL COOKING TIME: 15 MINUTES | SERVES 4

1 teaspoon sesame oil
1 tablespoon peanut oil
2 garlic cloves, crushed
1 tablespoon grated fresh ginger
1 red chilli, finely sliced
4 spring onions (scallions), sliced on
   the diagonal
300 g (10½ oz) tempeh, diced
500 g (1 lb 2 oz) baby bok choy (pak choy)
   leaves
800 g (1 lb 12 oz) Chinese broccoli, chopped
125 ml (4 fl oz/½ cup) mushroom oyster sauce
2 tablespoons rice vinegar
2 tablespoons coriander (cilantro) leaves
3 tablespoons toasted cashew nuts

1   Heat the oils in a wok over high heat, add the garlic, ginger, chilli and spring onion and cook for 1–2 minutes, or until the onion is soft. Add the tempeh and cook for 5 minutes, or until golden. Remove and keep warm.

2   Add half the greens and 1 tablespoon water to the wok and cook, covered, for 3–4 minutes, or until wilted. Remove and repeat with the remaining greens and more water.

3   Return the greens and tempeh to the wok, add the sauce and vinegar and warm through. Top with the coriander and cashew nuts. Serve with rice.

Stir-fry the garlic, ginger, chilli and spring onion for 1–2 minutes.

Add the tempeh to the wok and stir-fry for 5 minutes, or until golden.

NUTRITION PER SERVE
Protein 23 g; Fat 15 g; Carbohydrate 12 g; Dietary
Fibre 15 g; Cholesterol 0 mg; 2220 kJ (529 Cal)

Tuna in makrut sauce

PREPARATION TIME: 5 MINUTES | TOTAL COOKING TIME: 15 MINUTES | SERVES 4

375 ml (13 fl oz/1½ cups) pouring
    (whipping) cream
375 ml (13 fl oz/1½ cups) fish stock
12 makrut (kaffir lime) leaves, finely sliced
2 tablespoons peanut oil
4 small tuna steaks, cubed
1 kg (2 lb 4 oz/2½ bunches) baby bok choy
    (pak choy), halved
lime wedges, to serve

1 Place the cream, fish stock and makrut leaves
in a small saucepan over low heat. Boil for
15 minutes, stirring occasionally, or until the
sauce has reduced and thickened. Keep warm.

2 Meanwhile, heat a wok until very hot, add
the oil and swirl to coat the side. Add the tuna,
in batches if necessary, and stir-fry for 2 minutes,
or until seared on all sides but not cooked
through. Remove the tuna.

3 Add the bok choy to the wok and stir-fry
over high heat for 1–2 minutes, or until the
leaves begin to wilt. Add 1–2 teaspoons water,
if necessary, to assist wilting.

4 Place the bok choy and tuna on a serving plate
and pour on the sauce. Serve with lime wedges.

NUTRITION PER SERVE
Protein 68 g; Fat 55 g; Carbohydrate 6 g; Dietary
Fibre 20 g; Cholesterol 276 mg; 3300 kJ (788 Cal)

Place the cream, fish stock and makrut leaves in a
saucepan and simmer.

Quickly stir-fry the tuna until just seared on all sides
but not cooked through.

Add the bok choy to the wok and stir-fry until just
starting to wilt.

Asian greens with teriyaki tofu dressing

PREPARATION TIME: 15 MINUTES | TOTAL COOKING TIME: 20 MINUTES | SERVES 6

650 g (1 lb 7 oz) baby bok choy (pak choy)
500 g (1 lb 2 oz) choy sum
440 g (15½ oz) snake (yard-long) beans,
    topped and tailed
60 ml (2 fl oz/¼ cup) oil
1 onion, thinly sliced
60 g (2¼ oz/⅓ cup) soft brown sugar
½ teaspoon ground chilli
2 tablespoons grated fresh ginger
250 ml (9 fl oz/1 cup) teriyaki sauce
1 tablespoon sesame oil
600 g (1 lb 5 oz) silken firm tofu, drained

> NUTRITION PER SERVE
> Protein 19 g; Fat 11 g; Carbohydrate 20 g; Dietary
> Fibre 11 g; Cholesterol 1 mg; 1093 kJ (260 Cal)

1   Cut the the baby bok choy and choy sum widthways into thirds. Cut the beans into 10 cm (4 inch) lengths.

2   Heat a wok over high heat, add 1 tablespoon of the oil and swirl to coat the side. Cook the onion in batches for 3–5 minutes, or until crisp. Remove with a slotted spoon and drain on paper towels.

3   Heat 1 tablespoon of the oil in the wok, add half the greens and stir-fry for 2–3 minutes, or until wilted. Remove and keep warm. Repeat with the remaining oil and greens. Remove. Drain any liquid from the wok.

4   Add the combined sugar, chilli, ginger and teriyaki sauce to the wok and bring to the boil. Simmer for 1 minute. Add the sesame oil and tofu and simmer for 2 minutes, turning once— the tofu will break up. Divide the greens among serving plates, then top with the dressing. Sprinkle with the fried onion.

Cut the baby bok choy and choy sum widthways into thirds.

Cook the combined greens in two batches until the leaves are wilted.

Turn the tofu with a spatula halfway through cooking—it will break up.

Sweet and sour tofu

PREPARATION TIME: 15 MINUTES | TOTAL COOKING TIME: 20 MINUTES | SERVES 4

600 g (1 lb 5 oz) firm tofu
3–4 tablespoons soya bean oil
1 large carrot, cut into matchsticks
150 g (5½ oz/1⅔ cups) trimmed bean sprouts
   or soya bean sprouts
90 g (3¼ oz/1 cup) sliced button mushrooms
6–8 spring onions (scallions), cut diagonally
100 g (3½ oz) snow peas (mangetouts), cut in
   half diagonally
80 ml (2½ fl oz/⅓ cup) rice vinegar
2 tablespoons light soy sauce
1½ tablespoons caster (superfine) sugar
2 tablespoons tomato sauce (ketchup)
375 ml (13 fl oz/1½ cups) chicken or
   vegetable stock
1 tablespoon cornflour (cornstarch)

1   Cut the tofu in half horizontally, then cut into 16 triangles in total. Heat 2 tablespoons of the oil in a frying pan. Add the tofu in batches and cook over medium heat for 2 minutes on each side, or until crisp and golden. Drain on paper towels. Keep warm.

2   Wipe the pan clean and heat the remaining oil. Add the carrot, bean sprouts, mushrooms, spring onion and snow peas and stir-fry for 1 minute. Add the vinegar, soy sauce, sugar, tomato sauce and stock and cook for a further 1 minute.

3   Combine the cornflour with 2 tablespoons water. Add to the vegetable mixture and cook until the sauce thickens. Serve the tofu with the sauce poured over the top.

Cut the firm tofu slices into 16 triangles with a sharp knife.

Fry the tofu triangles on both sides until they are crisp and golden.

NUTRITION PER SERVE
Protein 15 g; Fat 16 g; Carbohydrate 17 g; Dietary Fibre 4 g; Cholesterol 0 mg; 1178 kJ (280 Cal)

Honey and black pepper beef

PREPARATION TIME: **15** MINUTES | TOTAL COOKING TIME: **10** MINUTES | SERVES 4

oil, for cooking
500 g (1 lb 2 oz) round steak, cut into
    thin strips
2 garlic cloves, crushed
1 onion, sliced
300 g (10½ oz) sugar snap peas
2 tablespoons honey
2 teaspoons soy sauce
2 tablespoons oyster sauce

1   Heat the wok until very hot, add
1 tablespoon of the oil and swirl it around to
coat the side. Stir-fry the beef in batches over
high heat. Remove and drain on paper towels.

2   Reheat the wok, add 1 tablespoon of the oil
and stir-fry the garlic, onion and peas until
softened. Remove from the wok and set aside.

3   Add the honey, soy sauce, oyster sauce and
3 teaspoons cracked black pepper to the wok.
Bring to the boil, then reduce the heat and
simmer for 3–4 minutes, or until the sauce
thickens slightly.

4   Increase the heat, return the meat and
vegetables to the wok, and toss for 2–3 minutes,
or until well combined and heated through.

NUTRITION PER SERVE
Protein 30 g; Fat 15 g; Carbohydrate 20 g; Dietary
Fibre 4.5 g; Cholesterol 70 mg; 1400 kJ (335 Cal)

Heat the wok before adding the oil, then add the oil and swirl to coat the side.

Once the beef is cooked, remove it from the wok and drain on paper towels.

Add the honey, soy sauce, oyster sauce and cracked black pepper and bring to the boil.

Five-spice beef with Asian mushrooms

PREPARATION TIME: 20 MINUTES + 10 MINUTES RESTING | TOTAL COOKING TIME: 30 MINUTES | SERVES 4

60 ml (2 fl oz/¼ cup) soy sauce
60 ml (2 fl oz/¼ cup) mirin
60 ml (2 fl oz/¼ cup) sake
2 tablespoons soft brown sugar
3 teaspoons five-spice
1 teaspoon sea salt flakes
4 fillet steaks
600 g (1 lb 5 oz) orange sweet
    potato, chopped
1 tablespoon butter
90 g (3¼ oz/⅓ cup) sour cream
2 garlic cloves, crushed
1 teaspoon ground ginger
1 tablespoon peanut oil
2 teaspoons butter, for pan-frying, extra
1 teaspoon grated fresh ginger
1 garlic clove, crushed, extra
100 g (3½ oz) shiitake mushrooms, sliced
100 g (3½ oz) shimeji mushrooms,
    pulled apart
100 g (3½ oz) enoki mushrooms
sesame seeds, toasted, to serve

1 Place the soy sauce, mirin, sake and sugar in a small saucepan and boil over high heat for 5 minutes, or until reduced and thickened slightly. Remove from the heat and cover.

2 Rub the combined five-spice and sea salt into the steaks.

3 Boil the orange sweet potato for 12 minutes, or until soft. Drain well, then add the butter, sour cream, garlic and ground ginger and mash together until smooth and creamy. Season, cover and keep warm.

4 Heat the oil in a large frying pan over high heat. When very hot, cook the steaks for 4–5 minutes each side for medium–rare, or until done to your liking. Remove from the pan, cover with foil and rest for 10 minutes.

5 Melt the extra butter in a frying pan over medium heat until just sizzling, then stir in the fresh ginger and extra garlic. Add the shiitake and shimeji mushrooms and stir for 3 minutes, or until wilted. Add the enoki mushrooms, remove from the heat, cover and keep warm. Reheat the sauce and sweet potato and serve with the steaks. Top with the mushrooms and sesame seeds.

NUTRITION PER SERVE
Protein 47 g; Fat 28 g; Carbohydrate 13 g; Dietary Fibre 2.5 g; Cholesterol 180 mg; 2105 kJ (505 Cal)

Boil the sauce over high heat until it has reduced and thickened slightly.

Cook the shiitake and shimeji mushrooms until they are wilted, then add the enoki mushrooms.

Peanut chicken with mango

PREPARATION TIME: 10 MINUTES | TOTAL COOKING TIME: 15 MINUTES | SERVES 4

80 ml (2½ fl oz/⅓ cup) ready-made satay sauce
125 ml (4 fl oz/½ cup) coconut cream
125 ml (4 fl oz/½ cup) chicken stock
2 teaspoons soy sauce
4 boneless, skinless chicken breasts, cut
    into strips
plain (all-purpose) flour, for coating
2 tablespoons oil
1 large ripe mango, sliced

1 Whisk together the satay sauce, coconut cream, stock and soy sauce.

2 Lightly coat the chicken with flour. Heat the oil in a large deep frying pan and cook the chicken over medium heat for 4–5 minutes, or until golden brown. Remove from the pan.

3 Add the satay sauce mixture to the pan and bring to the boil. Boil for 3–5 minutes, or until the sauce is reduced by half. Return the chicken to the pan and heat through for 1 minute. Serve the chicken over steamed rice, topped with mango slices.

NUTRITION PER SERVE
Protein 30 g; Fat 25 g; Carbohydrate 17 g; Dietary
Fibre 2 g; Cholesterol 70 mg; 1710 kJ (410 Cal)

Whisk together the satay sauce, coconut cream, chicken stock and soy sauce.

Lightly coat the chicken with flour and then cook in a frying pan until golden brown.

Return the chicken to the sauce and heat through for 1 minute.

Sesame-coated tuna with coriander salsa

PREPARATION TIME: 15 MINUTES + 15 MINUTES REFRIGERATION | TOTAL COOKING TIME: 10 MINUTES | SERVES 4

4 tuna steaks
120 g (4¼ oz/¾ cup) sesame seeds
100 g (3½ oz) baby rocket (arugula) leaves

CORIANDER SALSA
2 tomatoes, seeded and diced
1 large garlic clove, crushed
2 tablespoons finely chopped coriander
    (cilantro) leaves
2 tablespoons virgin olive oil, plus extra
    for shallow-frying
1 tablespoon lime juice

1 Cut each tuna steak into three pieces. Place the sesame seeds on a sheet of baking paper. Roll the tuna in the sesame seeds to coat. Refrigerate for 15 minutes.

2 To make the salsa, mix together the tomato, garlic, coriander, olive oil and lime juice. Cover and refrigerate.

3 Fill a heavy-based frying pan to 1.5 cm (⅝ inch) deep with the extra oil and place over high heat. Add the tuna in two batches and cook for 2 minutes each side. Remove and drain on paper towels. Divide the rocket among four plates, top with the tuna and serve with the salsa.

NUTRITION PER SERVE
Protein 26 g; Fat 36 g; Carbohydrate 2 g; Dietary
Fibre 2 g; Cholesterol 45 mg; 1696 kJ (403 Cal)

Put the sesame seeds on baking paper and roll the tuna in the seeds to coat.

Mix together the tomato, garlic, coriander, oil and lime juice to make a salsa.

Shallow fry the tuna for 2 minutes on each side or until it is cooked but still pink in the centre.

Chilli crab

PREPARATION TIME: 20 MINUTES | TOTAL COOKING TIME: 15 MINUTES | SERVES 4

1 kg (2 lb 4 oz) raw blue swimmer crabs
2 tablespoons peanut oil
2 garlic cloves, finely chopped
2 teaspoons finely chopped fresh ginger
2 small red chillies, seeded and sliced
    (see NOTE)
2 tablespoons hoisin sauce
125 ml (4 fl oz/½ cup) tomato
    sauce (ketchup)
60 ml (2 fl oz/¼ cup) sweet chilli sauce
1 tablespoon fish sauce
½ teaspoon sesame oil
4 spring onions (scallions), finely sliced, to
    garnish, optional

1   Pull back the apron and remove the top shell from each crab. Remove the intestines and grey feathery gills. Segment each crab into four pieces. Crack the claws open with a crab cracker to allow the flavours to enter the crabmeat and also to make it easier to eat the crab.

2   Heat a wok until very hot, add the oil and swirl to coat. Add the garlic, ginger and chilli and stir-fry for 1–2 minutes.

3   Add the crab pieces and stir-fry for 5–7 minutes, or until the meat turns white. Stir in the hoisin, tomato, sweet chilli and fish sauces, the sesame oil and 60 ml (2 fl oz/¼ cup) water. Bring to the boil, then reduce the heat and simmer, covered, for 6 minutes, or until the crab flesh is cooked through and flakes easily. Garnish with spring onion and serve with finger bowls.

VARIATION: *You can use any variety of raw crabmeat for this recipe, or use prawns (shrimp) instead.*

NOTE: *If you prefer a hotter sauce, leave the seeds and membrane in the chillies.*

NUTRITION PER SERVE
Protein 17 g; Fat 12 g; Carbohydrate 19 g; Dietary Fibre 3 g; Cholesterol 105 mg; 1045 kJ (250 Cal)

Pull the apron back from the crabs and remove the top shell from each.

Pull out and discard the intestines and grey feathery gills.

Use a sharp strong knife to cut each crab into 4 pieces.

Barbecued pork and broccoli

PREPARATION TIME: 25 MINUTES | TOTAL COOKING TIME: 10 MINUTES | SERVES 4–6

1 tablespoon oil
1 large onion, thinly sliced
2 carrots, cut into matchsticks
200 g (7 oz) broccoli, cut into bite-sized florets
6 spring onions (scallions), diagonally sliced
1 tablespoon finely chopped fresh ginger
3 garlic cloves, finely chopped
400 g (14 oz) Chinese barbecued pork
    (char siu), thinly sliced (see NOTE)
2 tablespoons soy sauce
2 tablespoons mirin
180 g (6¼ oz/2 cups) bean sprouts

1   Heat the wok until very hot, add the oil and swirl it around to coat the side. Stir-fry the onion over medium heat for 3–4 minutes, or until slightly softened. Add the carrot, broccoli, spring onion, ginger and garlic, and stir-fry for 4–5 minutes.

2   Increase the heat to high and add the barbecued pork. Toss constantly until the pork is well mixed with the vegetables and is heated through. Add the soy sauce and mirin, and toss until the ingredients are well coated. (The wok should be hot enough that the sauce reduces a little to form a glaze-like consistency.) Add the bean sprouts and season well with salt and pepper. Serve immediately.

NOTE: *Chinese barbecued pork is available from Asian stores.*

Peel the carrots, if necessary, and cut them into even-sized matchsticks.

Cut the pieces of Chinese barbecued pork into thin slices.

NUTRITION PER SERVE (6)
Protein 20 g; Fat 15 g; Carbohydrate 6.5 g; Dietary Fibre 6 g; Cholesterol 40 mg; 920 kJ (220 Cal)

Salmon with Asian greens and chilli jam

PREPARATION TIME: 20 MINUTES | TOTAL COOKING TIME: 1 HOUR | SERVES 4

CHILLI JAM
2½ tablespoons vegetable oil
1 large onion, thinly sliced
6 red bird's eye chillies, seeded and
    thinly sliced
2 teaspoons grated fresh ginger
185 ml (6 fl oz/¾ cup) white wine vinegar
150 g (5½ oz/¾ cup) soft brown sugar
2 teaspoons lime juice

1 tablespoon peanut oil
1 red capsicum (pepper), thinly sliced
500 g (1 lb 2 oz/1½ bunch) baby bok choy
    (pak choy), quartered
1 garlic clove, finely chopped
1 tablespoon soy sauce
1 teaspoon sugar
1 tablespoon oil
4 salmon cutlets

1   To make the chilli jam, heat the oil in a saucepan and add the onion, chilli and ginger. Cook over medium heat for 3–4 minutes, or until the onion is soft. Add the remaining ingredients and 60 ml (2 fl oz/¼ cup) water and stir until the sugar dissolves. Bring to the boil, then reduce the heat and simmer for 35–40 minutes, or until thick and pulpy. Cool slightly and mix until smooth in a food processor. Cool.

2   Heat the peanut oil in a frying pan, add the capsicum and cook over medium heat for 2 minutes, then add the bok choy and cook for 1 minute. Add the garlic and cook until fragrant. Reduce the heat, add the soy sauce and sugar and warm. Remove from the heat. Keep warm.

3   Heat the oil in a frying pan, season the salmon and cook over medium heat for 2 minutes each side, or until cooked to your liking. Serve with the vegetables and jam.

NUTRITION PER SERVE
Protein 50 g; Fat 27 g; Carbohydrate 40 g; Dietary Fibre 6.5 g; Cholesterol 140 mg; 2513 kJ (600 Cal)

Simmer the chilli jam until it thickens and becomes pulpy.

Cook the seasoned salmon cutlets, taking care not to overcook or the flesh will be dry.

Sweet and sour pork

PREPARATION TIME: 25 MINUTES + 30 MINUTES MARINATING | TOTAL COOKING TIME: 20 MINUTES | SERVES 4

500 g (1 lb 2 oz) pork fillet, cut into
     thick slices
2 tablespoons cornflour (cornstarch)
1 tablespoon sherry
1 tablespoon soy sauce
1 tablespoon sugar
oil, for cooking
1 large onion, thinly sliced
1 green capsicum (pepper), cut into squares
2 small carrots, thinly sliced
1 small Lebanese (short) cucumber, seeded
     and chopped
5 spring onions (scallions), cut into
     short lengths
440 g (15½ oz) tin pineapple pieces in natural
     juice, drained and juice reserved
60 ml (2 fl oz/¼ cup) white vinegar

NUTRITION PER SERVE
Protein 25 g; Fat 12 g; Carbohydrate 25 g; Dietary
Fibre 4 g; Cholesterol 50 mg; 1325 kJ (315 Cal)

1   Place the pork in a shallow glass or ceramic bowl. Combine the cornflour with the sherry, soy sauce and half the sugar, and pour into the bowl. Cover and refrigerate for 30 minutes.

2   Drain the pork, reserving the marinade. Heat the wok until very hot, add 2 tablespoons of the oil and swirl to coat the side. Stir-fry half the pork over high heat for 4–5 minutes, or until the pork is golden brown and just cooked. Remove from the wok, add more oil if necessary and repeat with the remaining pork. Remove all the pork from the wok.

3   Reheat the wok, add 1 tablespoon of the oil and stir-fry the onion over high heat for 3–4 minutes, or until slightly softened. Add the capsicum and carrot, and cook for 3–4 minutes, or until tender. Stir in the marinade, cucumber, spring onion, pineapple, vinegar, ½ teaspoon salt, remaining sugar and 80 ml (2½ fl oz/ ⅓ cup) of the pineapple juice.

4   Bring to the boil and simmer for 2–3 minutes, or until the sauce has thickened slightly. Return the pork to the wok and toss to heat through.

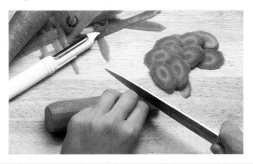
Peel the carrots, if necessary, and cut them into thin diagonal slices.

Halve the cucumber lengthways and scoop out the seeds using a teaspoon.

Stir-fry the pork until it is golden brown and just cooked, then remove from the wok.

Mongolian lamb

PREPARATION TIME: 15 MINUTES | TOTAL COOKING TIME: 12 MINUTES | SERVES 4

oil, for cooking
500 g (1 lb 2 oz) lamb backstrap (tender eye of
    the lamb loin), cut into thin strips
2 garlic cloves, crushed
4 spring onions (scallions), thickly sliced
2 tablespoons soy sauce
80 ml (2½ fl oz/⅓ cup) dry sherry
2 tablespoons sweet chilli sauce
2 teaspoons sesame seeds, toasted

1 Heat the wok until very hot, add
1 tablespoon of the oil and swirl it around to coat
the side. Stir-fry the lamb strips in batches over
high heat. Remove all the lamb from the wok.

2 Reheat the wok, add 1 tablespoon of oil and
stir-fry the garlic and spring onion for 2 minutes.
Remove from the wok and set aside. Add the soy
sauce, sherry and sweet chilli sauce to the wok.
Bring to the boil, reduce the heat and simmer for
3–4 minutes, or until the sauce thickens slightly.

3 Return the meat, with any juices, and
the garlic and spring onion to the wok, and
toss to coat. Serve sprinkled with the toasted
sesame seeds.

NUTRITION PER SERVE
Protein 30 g; Fat 20 g; Carbohydrate 7 g; Dietary
Fibre 1.5 g; Cholesterol 80 mg; 1445 kJ (345 Cal)

Slice the lamb backstrap into thin strips with a
sharp knife.

Stir-fry the lamb strips in batches over high heat
and then remove from the wok.

Add the soy sauce, sherry and sweet chilli sauce to
the wok, and bring to the boil.

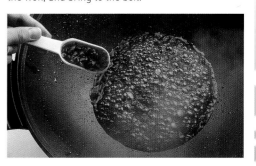

Coriander and lime chicken

PREPARATION TIME: 10 MINUTES | TOTAL COOKING TIME: 15 MINUTES | SERVES 4

170 ml (5½ fl oz/⅔ cup) coconut cream
125 ml (4 fl oz/½ cup) chicken stock
1½ tablespoons lime juice
2 teaspoons grated fresh ginger
4 boneless, skinless chicken breasts, cut
   into strips
plain (all-purpose) flour, for coating
2 tablespoons oil
2 tablespoons chopped coriander (cilantro)
   leaves, plus extra to garnish

1 Whisk together the coconut cream, stock, lime juice and ginger. Lightly coat the chicken with flour.

2 Heat the oil in a frying pan and cook the chicken over medium heat for 4–5 minutes, or until golden brown. Remove from the pan and keep warm. Add the coconut cream mixture to the pan and bring to the boil. Cook for 5 minutes, or until reduced by half and thickened slightly.

3 Return the chicken to the pan, add the coriander and simmer for 1 minute to heat the chicken through. Garnish with extra coriander leaves.

NUTRITION PER SERVE
Protein 50 g; Fat 20 g; Carbohydrate 13 g; Dietary
Fibre 1 g; Cholesterol 110 mg; 1785 kJ (425 Cal)

Whisk together the coconut cream, stock, lime juice and ginger.

Boil the coconut cream, stock, lime juice and ginger until reduced and thickened.

Return the chicken to the pan, add the coriander and simmer to heat through.

Chicken and cashew nuts

PREPARATION TIME: 30 MINUTES | TOTAL COOKING TIME: 20 MINUTES | SERVES 4–6

oil, for cooking

750 g (1 lb 10 oz) boneless, skinless chicken
    thighs, cut into strips

2 egg whites, lightly beaten

60 g (2¼ oz/½ cup) cornflour (cornstarch)

2 onions, thinly sliced

1 red capsicum (pepper), thinly sliced

200 g (7 oz) broccoli, cut into
    bite-sized pieces

2 tablespoons soy sauce

2 tablespoons sherry

1 tablespoon oyster sauce

50 g (1¾ oz/⅓ cup) roasted cashew nuts

4 spring onions (scallions), sliced diagonally

NUTRITION PER SERVE (6)
Protein 35 g; Fat 15 g; Carbohydrate 15 g; Dietary
Fibre 3 g; Cholesterol 60 mg; 1375 kJ (330 Cal)

1 Heat the wok until very hot, add 1 tablespoon of the oil and swirl it around to coat the side. Dip about a quarter of the chicken strips into the egg white and then into the cornflour. Add to the wok and stir-fry for 3–5 minutes, or until the chicken is golden brown and just cooked. Drain on paper towels and repeat with the remaining chicken, reheating the wok and adding a little more oil each time.

2 Reheat the wok, add 1 tablespoon of the oil and stir-fry the onion, capsicum and broccoli over medium heat for 4–5 minutes, or until the vegetables have softened slightly. Increase the heat to high and add the soy sauce, sherry and oyster sauce. Toss the vegetables well in the sauce and bring to the boil.

3 Return the chicken to the wok and toss over high heat for 1–2 minutes to heat the chicken and make sure it is entirely cooked through. Season well with salt and freshly cracked black pepper. Toss the cashews and spring onion through the chicken mixture, and serve immediately.

Dip the chicken strips into the egg white, then into the cornflour.

Stir-fry the chicken in batches until it is golden brown and just cooked.

Honey chicken

PREPARATION TIME: 15 MINUTES | TOTAL COOKING TIME: 25 MINUTES | SERVES 4

oil, for cooking
500 g (1 lb 2 oz) boneless, skinless chicken
　　thighs, cut into cubes
1 egg white, lightly beaten
40 g (1½ oz/⅓ cup) cornflour (cornstarch)
2 onions, thinly sliced
1 green capsicum (pepper), cut into squares
2 carrots, cut into batons
100 g (3½ oz/1 cup) snow peas (mangetouts),
　　sliced
90 g (3¼ oz/¼ cup) honey
2 tablespoons almonds, toasted

1　Heat the wok until very hot, add
1½ tablespoons of the oil and swirl it around to
coat the side. Dip half of the chicken into the egg
white, then lightly dust with the cornflour. Stir-
fry over high heat for 4–5 minutes, or until the
chicken is golden brown and just cooked.
Remove from the wok and drain on paper
towels. Repeat with the remaining chicken, then
remove all the chicken from the wok.

2　Reheat the wok, add 1 tablespoon of the oil
and stir-fry the sliced onion over high heat for
3–4 minutes, or until slightly softened. Add the
capsicum and carrot, and cook, tossing
constantly, for 3–4 minutes, or until tender. Stir
in the snow peas and cook for 2 minutes.

3　Increase the heat, add the honey and toss the
vegetables until well coated. Return the chicken
to the wok and toss until it is heated through and
is well coated in the honey. Remove from the
heat and season well with salt and pepper. Serve
immediately, sprinkled with the almonds.

Trim the excess fat from the chicken and cut the
chicken into cubes.

Dip the chicken into the egg white, then lightly dust
with the cornflour.

NUTRITION PER SERVE
Protein 35 g; Fat 20 g; Carbohydrate 35 g; Dietary
Fibre 4 g; Cholesterol 60 mg; 1815 kJ (435 Cal)

Teriyaki tuna with wasabi mayonnaise

PREPARATION TIME: 10 MINUTES + 10 MINUTES MARINATING | TOTAL COOKING TIME: 10 MINUTES | SERVES 4

125 ml (4 fl oz/½ cup) teriyaki marinade
½ teaspoon five-spice
1 tablespoon grated fresh ginger
3 tuna steaks, each cut into 4 strips
2 tablespoons peanut oil
60 g (2¼ oz/¼ cup) mayonnaise
1 teaspoon wasabi paste
2 tablespoons pickled ginger, to serve

1   Combine the teriyaki marinade, five-spice powder and ginger. Place the tuna in a non-metallic dish, pour over the marinade, cover and leave to marinate for 10 minutes. Drain and discard the marinade.

2   Heat the oil in a large non-stick frying pan. Add the tuna, in batches if necessary, and cook over high heat for 1–2 minutes each side, or until cooked to your liking. The time will vary depending on the thickness of the fish.

3   Mix together the mayonnaise and wasabi paste. Serve the tuna steaks with wasabi mayonnaise and a little pickled ginger.

NUTRITION PER SERVE
Protein 27 g; Fat 17 g; Carbohydrate 4 g; Dietary Fibre 0 g; Cholesterol 50 mg; 1196 kJ (284 Cal)

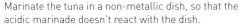

Marinate the tuna in a non-metallic dish, so that the acidic marinade doesn't react with the dish.

Cook the tuna, in batches if necessary, over high heat until cooked to your liking.

Mix together the mayonnaise and wasabi paste to make a hot dressing.

Beef and hokkien noodles

PREPARATION TIME: 15 MINUTES + 10 MINUTES SOAKING | TOTAL COOKING TIME: 15 MINUTES | SERVES 4

350 g (12 oz) beef fillet, partially frozen
   (see HINT)
100 g (3½ oz) snow peas (mangetouts)
600 g (1 lb 5 oz) fresh hokkien (egg) noodles
2 tablespoons peanut oil
1 large onion, cut into thin wedges
1 large carrot, sliced thinly on the diagonal
1 red capsicum (pepper), cut into thin strips
2 garlic cloves, crushed
1 teaspoon grated fresh ginger
200 g (7 oz) shiitake mushrooms, sliced
60 ml (2 fl oz/¼ cup) oyster sauce
2 tablespoons light soy sauce
1 tablespoon soft brown sugar
½ teaspoon five-spice

NUTRITION PER SERVE
Protein 38 g; Fat 10 g; Carbohydrate 92 g; Dietary
Fibre 7 g; Cholesterol 78 mg; 2555 kJ (610 Cal)

1 Cut the steak into thin slices. Top and tail the snow peas and slice in half diagonally. Soak the noodles in a large bowl of boiling water for 10 minutes.

2 Heat a wok to very hot, add half the peanut oil and stir-fry the steak in batches until brown. Remove.

3 Heat the remaining peanut oil in the wok until very hot and stir-fry the onion, carrot and capsicum for 2–3 minutes, or until tender. Add the garlic, ginger, snow peas and shiitake mushrooms and cook for another minute. Return the steak to the wok.

4 Separate the noodles with a fork, then drain. Add to the wok, tossing well. Combine the oyster sauce with the soy sauce, brown sugar, five-spice and 1 tablespoon water and pour over the noodles. Toss until warmed through.

HINT: *Partially freezing the meat will firm it up and make it easier to slice thinly.*

Cut the partially frozen beef fillet into thin slices with a sharp knife.

Add the garlic, ginger, snow peas and shiitake mushrooms and cook for another minute.

Teppan yaki

PREPARATION TIME: 45 MINUTES | TOTAL COOKING TIME: 25 MINUTES | SERVES 4

350 g (12 oz) beef fillet, partially frozen
4 small slender eggplants (aubergines)
100 g (3½ oz) fresh shiitake mushrooms
100 g (3½ oz) baby green beans
6 yellow or green baby (pattypan) squash
1 red or green capsicum (pepper), seeded
6 spring onions (scallions)
200 g (7 oz) tinned bamboo shoots, drained
3 tablespoons vegetable oil
soy and ginger dipping sauce

1   Slice the steak very thinly. Mark a large cross on each slice of meat. Place the slices in a single layer and season well.

2   Trim the ends from the eggplants and cut the flesh into long, very thin diagonal slices. Trim any tough stalks from the mushrooms and top and tail the beans. Quarter or halve the squash, depending on the size. Cut the capsicum into thin strips and slice the spring onions into long pieces. Trim the bamboo shoot slices to a similar size. Arrange the vegetables in separate bundles.

3   Heat an electric grill or electric frying pan until very hot and then lightly brush it with the oil. Quickly fry about a quarter of the meat, searing on both sides, and then move it over to the edge of the pan. Add about a quarter of the vegetables to the grill or pan and quickly stir-fry, adding a little more oil as needed. Serve a small portion of the meat and vegetables to each guest with sauces for dipping.

Using a sharp knife, make a large cross on each slice of meat.

Sear the meat quickly on each side, using tongs to turn it.

NUTRITION PER SERVE
Protein 25 g; Fat 20 g; Carbohydrate 8 g; Dietary
Fibre 6 g; Cholesterol 60 mg; 1220 kJ (290 Cal)

Hoisin pork with stir-fried greens

PREPARATION TIME: 15 MINUTES + 10 MINUTES STANDING | TOTAL COOKING TIME: 35 MINUTES | SERVES 4

250 g (9 oz/1¼ cups) jasmine rice
500 g (1 lb 2 oz) pork fillet, thinly sliced
1 tablespoon caster (superfine) sugar
2 tablespoons oil
125 ml (4 fl oz/½ cup) white wine vinegar
250 ml (9 fl oz/1 cup) hoisin sauce
2 tablespoons stem ginger in syrup, chopped
    (see NOTE)
1.25 kg (2 lb 12 oz) mixed Asian greens, such
    as bok choy (pak choy), choy sum
    or spinach

1 Rinse the rice and place in a large saucepan. Add 435 ml (15¼ fl oz/1¾ cups) water and bring to the boil. Cover, reduce the heat to very low and cook for 10 minutes. Remove from the heat and leave to stand, covered, for 10 minutes. Meanwhile, place the pork in a bowl and sprinkle with the sugar. Toss to coat. Heat a wok over high heat, add 1 tablespoon oil and swirl to coat. Add the pork in batches and stir-fry for 3 minutes, or until brown. Remove all the pork from the wok. Add the vinegar to the wok and boil for 3–5 minutes, or until reduced by two-thirds. Reduce the heat, add the hoisin sauce and 1 tablespoon ginger, and simmer for 5 minutes.

2 Reheat the wok over high heat, add the remaining oil and swirl to coat. Add the greens and stir-fry for 3 minutes, or until crisp and cooked. Stir the remaining ginger through the rice, then press into four round teacups or small Asian bowls, smoothing the surface. Unmould the rice onto four serving plates, arrange the pork and greens on the side and drizzle the sauce over the top.

NOTE: *Stem ginger is available from Asian food stores. Substitute glacé (candied) ginger if it is unavailable.*

Sprinkle the pork with sugar and then stir-fry until it is brown.

Press the gingered rice into teacups or small Asian bowls to give it a neat shape.

NUTRITION PER SERVE
Protein 50 g; Fat 17 g; Carbohydrate 177 g; Dietary Fibre 20 g; Cholesterol 60 mg; 4523 kJ (1080 Cal)

Squid in black bean and chilli sauce

PREPARATION TIME: 20 MINUTES | TOTAL COOKING TIME: 10 MINUTES | SERVES 4

4 squid tubes
2 tablespoons oil
1 onion, cut into wedges
1 red capsicum (pepper), sliced
120 g (4¼ oz) baby corn, halved
3 spring onions (scallions), cut into
    short lengths

BLACK BEAN SAUCE
3 teaspoons cornflour (cornstarch)
2 tablespoons canned salted black beans,
    rinsed (see NOTE)
2 small red chillies, seeded and chopped
2 garlic cloves, finely chopped
2 teaspoons grated fresh ginger
2 tablespoons oyster sauce
2 teaspoons soy sauce
1 teaspoon sugar

1 Open out the squid tubes. Lightly score a diamond pattern over the inside surface of each, then cut into 5 cm (2 inch) squares.

2 For the sauce, mix the cornflour with 125 ml (4 fl oz/½ cup) water. Mash the black beans with a fork. Add the chilli, garlic, ginger, oyster and soy sauces, sugar and the cornflour mixture and stir well.

3 Heat the oil in a wok or frying pan and stir-fry the onion for 1 minute over high heat. Add the capsicum and corn and cook for another 2 minutes.

4 Add the squid to the wok and stir for 1–2 minutes, until it curls up. Add the sauce and bring to the boil, stirring until the sauce thickens. Stir in the spring onion.

VARIATION: *Instead of squid, you can use fish, cuttlefish, prawns (shrimp) or octopus.*

NOTE: *Black beans are available in cans in Asian food stores.*

NUTRITION PER SERVE
Protein 12 g; Fat 11 g; Carbohydrate 13 g; Dietary
Fibre 3.5 g; Cholesterol 100 mg; 800 kJ (190 Cal)

Score a shallow diamond pattern over the inside surface of each squid tube.

The squid are cooked when they start to curl up. Don't overcook them or they'll be tough.

Add the sauce, bring to the boil and stir constantly until the sauce thickens.

Chicken with snow pea sprouts

PREPARATION TIME: 15 MINUTES I TOTAL COOKING TIME: 15 MINUTES I SERVES 4

2 tablespoons oil
1 onion, finely sliced
3 makrut (kaffir lime) leaves, shredded
3 boneless, skinless chicken breasts, diced
1 red capsicum (pepper), sliced
60 ml (2 fl oz/¼ cup) lime juice
100 ml (3½ fl oz) soy sauce
100 g (3½ oz) snow pea (mangetout) sprouts
2 tablespoons chopped coriander (cilantro)
    leaves

1 Heat a wok or frying pan over medium heat, add the oil and swirl to coat. Add the onion and makrut leaves and stir-fry for 3–5 minutes, or until the onion begins to soften. Add the chicken and cook for a further 4 minutes. Add the capsicum and continue to cook for 2–3 minutes.

2 Stir in the lime juice and soy sauce and cook for 1–2 minutes, or until the sauce reduces slightly. Add the sprouts and coriander and cook until the sprouts have wilted slightly.

VARIATION: *Use the chicken, soy sauce and lime juice as a base and add fresh asparagus, or use mint and basil instead of coriander.*

Cook the chicken for 4 minutes and then add the capsicum to the wok.

Add the snow pea sprouts and coriander and cook until the sprouts wilt slightly.

NUTRITION PER SERVE
Protein 45 g; Fat 15 g; Carbohydrate 5.5 g; Dietary Fibre 2 g; Cholesterol 90 mg; 1375 kJ (330 Cal)

Tonkatsu

PREPARATION TIME: 35 MINUTES + 2 HOURS REFRIGERATION I TOTAL COOKING TIME: 12 MINUTES I SERVES 4

500 g (1 lb 2 oz) pork loin
60 g (2¼ oz/½ cup) plain (all-purpose) flour
6 egg yolks, beaten with 2 tablespoons water
120 g (4¼ oz/2 cups) Japanese dried
    breadcrumbs (panko)
2 spring onions (scallions)
pickled ginger and pickled daikon
90 g (3¼ oz/2 cups) finely shredded Chinese
    or savoy cabbage
1 sheet nori (dried seaweed)
375 ml (13 fl oz/1½ cups) oil
250 ml (9 fl oz/1 cup) tonkatsu sauce

1 Cut the pork into 8 thin slices. Sprinkle with salt and pepper and lightly coat with flour.

2 Dip the pork in the egg and then the breadcrumbs, pressing the crumbs on with your fingertips for an even coating. Arrange in a single layer on a plate and refrigerate, uncovered, for at least 2 hours.

3 To prepare the garnishes, peel away the outside layers of the spring onions, then slice the stems very finely and place in a bowl of cold water until serving time. Slice the ginger and daikon and set aside with the shredded cabbage. Using a sharp knife, shred the nori very finely and then break into strips about 4 cm (1½ inches) long.

4 Heat the oil in a heavy-based frying pan. Cook 2–3 pork steaks at a time until golden brown on both sides, then drain on kitchen towels. Slice the pork into strips and reassemble into the original steak shape. Top each one with a few nori strips. Serve with the tonkatsu sauce, shredded cabbage, drained spring onions, pickled ginger, daikon and steamed rice.

Use your fingertips to press the breadcrumbs onto the pork.

Shred the nori finely, and then break it into strips about 4 cm long.

NUTRITION PER SERVE
Protein 40 g; Fat 25 g; Carbohydrate 42 g; Dietary Fibre 3 g; Cholesterol 325 mg; 2320 kJ (555 Cal)

Tofu in black bean sauce

PREPARATION TIME: 20 MINUTES I TOTAL COOKING TIME: 15 MINUTES I SERVES 4

80 ml (2½ fl oz/⅓ cup) vegetable stock
2 teaspoons cornflour (cornstarch)
2 teaspoons Chinese rice wine (see NOTE)
1 teaspoon sesame oil
1 tablespoon soy sauce
2 tablespoons peanut oil
450 g (1 lb) firm tofu, cubed
2 garlic cloves, very finely chopped
2 teaspoons finely chopped fresh ginger
3 tablespoons fermented black beans, rinsed
    and very finely chopped
4 spring onions (scallions), cut on
    the diagonal
1 red capsicum (pepper), cut into squares
300 g (10½ oz) baby bok choy
    (pak choy), chopped

NUTRITION PER SERVE
Protein 13 g; Fat 14 g; Carbohydrate 4 g; Dietary
Fibre 4 g; Cholesterol 0 mg; 850 kJ (205 Cal)

1 Combine the vegetable stock, cornflour, rice wine, sesame oil, soy sauce, ½ teaspoon salt and freshly ground black pepper in a small bowl.

2 Heat a wok over medium heat, add the peanut oil and swirl to coat. Add the tofu and stir-fry in two batches for 3 minutes each batch, or until lightly browned. Remove with a slotted spoon and drain on paper towels. Discard any bits of tofu stuck to the wok or floating in the oil.

3 Add the garlic and ginger and stir-fry for 30 seconds. Toss in the black beans and spring onion and stir-fry for 30 seconds. Add the capsicum and stir-fry for 1 minute. Add the bok choy and stir-fry for a further 2 minutes. Return the tofu to the wok and stir gently. Pour in the sauce and stir gently for 2–3 minutes, or until the sauce has thickened slightly. Serve immediately.

NOTE: *Chinese rice wine is an alcoholic liquid made from cooked glutinous rice and millet mash which has been fermented with yeast, then aged for a period of 10 to 100 years. With a sherry-like taste, it is used as both a drink and a cooking liquid.*

Stir-fry the tofu cubes in batches until they are lightly browned.

Stir-fry the garlic, ginger, black beans and spring onion.

Return the tofu to the wok and gently stir together with the vegetables.

Grilled and steamed

Beef teriyaki with cucumber salad

PREPARATION TIME: 20 MINUTES + 30 MINUTES REFRIGERATION | TOTAL COOKING TIME: 20 MINUTES | SERVES 4

4 fillet steaks
80 ml (2½ fl oz/⅓ cup) soy sauce
2 tablespoons mirin
1 tablespoon sake (optional)
1 garlic clove, crushed
1 teaspoon grated fresh ginger
1 teaspoon sugar
1 teaspoon toasted sesame seeds

CUCUMBER SALAD
1 large Lebanese (short) cucumber, peeled,
    seeded and diced
½ red capsicum (pepper), diced
2 spring onions (scallions), sliced thinly
2 teaspoons sugar
1 tablespoon rice wine vinegar

NUTRITION PER SERVE
Protein 23 g; Fat 5 g; Carbohydrate 6 g; Dietary
Fibre 1 g; Cholesterol 67 mg; 720 kJ (170 Cal)

1   Put the steaks in a non-metallic dish. Combine the soy sauce, mirin, sake, garlic and ginger and pour over the steaks. Cover with plastic wrap and refrigerate for at least 30 minutes.

2   Put the cucumber, capsicum and spring onion in a bowl. Put the sugar, rice wine vinegar and 60 ml (2 fl oz/¼ cup) water in a saucepan and stir over heat until the sugar dissolves. Increase the heat and simmer rapidly for 3–4 minutes, or until thickened. Pour over the cucumber salad, stir well and leave to cool completely.

3   Brush a chargrill plate or barbecue grill plate with oil and heat until very hot. Drain the steaks and reserve the marinade. Cook for 3–4 minutes on each side, or to your taste. Rest the meat for 5–10 minutes before slicing.

4   Put the sugar and reserved marinade in a saucepan and heat, stirring, until the sugar has dissolved. Bring to the boil, then simmer for 2–3 minutes.

5   Slice each steak into strips and serve with the marinade, cucumber salad and a sprinkling of sesame seeds.

Combine the cucumber, capsicum and spring onion with the dressing.

Cook the steaks for 3–4 minutes on each side, or until they are cooked to your taste.

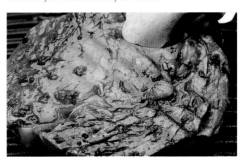

Lemongrass and coriander fish

PREPARATION TIME: 15 MINUTES | TOTAL COOKING TIME: 40 MINUTES | SERVES 4

4 x 200 g (7 oz) fish cutlets
plain (all-purpose) flour, seasoned with salt
    and pepper
2–3 tablespoons peanut oil
2 onions, sliced
2 lemongrass stems, white part only,
    finely chopped
4 makrut (kaffir lime) leaves, finely shredded
1 teaspoon ground cumin
1 teaspoon ground coriander
1 teaspoon finely chopped red chilli
185 ml (6 fl oz/¾ cup) chicken stock
375 ml (13 fl oz/1½ cups) coconut milk
1 very large handful fresh coriander
    (cilantro), chopped
2 teaspoons fish sauce

1 Preheat the oven to 180°C (350°F/Gas 4). Toss the fish lightly in the flour. Heat half the oil in a large heavy-based frying pan and cook the fish over medium heat until lightly browned on both sides. Transfer to a shallow ovenproof dish.

2 Heat the remaining oil in the pan. Add the onion and lemongrass and cook, stirring, for 5 minutes, or until the onion softens. Add the makrut leaves, ground spices and chilli and stir for about 2 minutes, or until fragrant.

3 Add the stock and coconut milk and bring to the boil. Pour over the fish, then cover and bake for 30 minutes, or until tender. Transfer to a plate.

4 Stir the coriander and fish sauce into the remaining sauce and season to taste. Pour over the fish to serve.

NOTE: *Makrut leaves are glossy, dark green double leaves with a floral citrus smell. They are tough and need to be finely shredded before use.*

Finely chop the white part of the lemongrass stems and shred the makrut leaves.

Heat half the peanut oil and brown the lightly floured fish over medium heat.

NUTRITION PER SERVE
Protein 35 g; Fat 40 g; Carbohydrate 6 g; Dietary
Fibre 1 g; Cholesterol 105 mg; 2040 kJ (490 Cal)

Thai drumsticks

PREPARATION TIME: 10 MINUTES + AT LEAST 2 HOURS MARINATING | TOTAL COOKING TIME: 30 MINUTES | SERVES 6

3 tablespoons Thai red curry paste
250 ml (9 fl oz/1 cup) coconut milk
2 tablespoons lime juice
4 tablespoons finely chopped coriander
    (cilantro) leaves
12 chicken drumsticks, scored
1 kg (2 lb 4 oz/2½ bunches) baby bok choy
    (pak choy)
2 tablespoons soy sauce
1 tablespoon oil

1   Mix together the curry paste, coconut milk, lime juice and coriander. Place the chicken in a non-metallic dish and pour on the marinade. Cover and leave in the refrigerator for at least 2 hours.

2   Cook the chicken over medium heat on a barbecue grill plate or flat plate for 25 minutes, or until cooked through.

3   Trim the bok choy and combine with the soy sauce and oil, then cook on the barbecue or in a frying pan for 3–4 minutes, or until just wilted. Serve the chicken on a bed of bok choy.

NUTRITION PER SERVE
Protein 30 g; Fat 20 g; Carbohydrate 3 g; Dietary Fibre 5 g; Cholesterol 105 mg; 1250 kJ (300 Cal)

Put the chicken in a non-metallic dish with the marinade and leave for 2 hours.

Cook the chicken on a barbecue grill plate or flat plate for 25 minutes, or until cooked through.

Cook the bok choy, soy sauce on the barbecue or in a frying pan until wilted.

Prawns steamed in banana leaves

PREPARATION TIME: 30 MINUTES + 2 HOURS MARINATING | TOTAL COOKING TIME: 15 MINUTES | SERVES 4

2.5 cm (1 inch) piece fresh ginger, grated
2 small red chillies, finely chopped
4 spring onions (scallions), finely chopped
2 lemongrass stems, white part only,
    finely chopped
2 teaspoons soft brown sugar
1 tablespoon fish sauce
2 tablespoons lime juice
1 tablespoon sesame seeds, toasted
2 tablespoons chopped coriander (cilantro)
1 kg (2 lb 4 oz) raw prawns (shrimp), peeled
    and deveined
8 small banana leaves (see NOTES)

1 Process the ginger, chillies, spring onion and lemongrass in a food processor, in short bursts, until the mixture forms a paste. Transfer the paste to a bowl, stir in the sugar, fish sauce, lime juice, sesame seeds and coriander and mix well. Add the prawns and toss to coat. Cover, refrigerate and marinate for 2 hours.

2 Soak the banana leaves in boiling water for 3 minutes to soften. Drain, pat dry and use scissors to cut them into eight squares of about 18 cm (7 inches).

3 Divide the prawn mixture into eight, place a portion onto each banana leaf, fold the leaf up to enclose the mixture and then secure the parcels, using a bamboo skewer.

4 Cook the parcels in a bamboo steamer over simmering water for 8–10 minutes, or until the prawn filling is cooked.

NOTES: *Banana leaves are available from Asian food stores and speciality fruit and vegetable shops. If banana leaves are not available, the prawn mixture can be wrapped in aluminium foil or baking paper and steamed. If you are cooking them on a barbecue, use foil.*

The parcels can also be cooked on the barbecue.

STORAGE: *The filled parcels can be made up a day in advance and stored, covered, in the refrigerator.*

NUTRITION PER SERVE
Protein 60 g; Fat 8 g; Carbohydrate 8 g; Dietary
Fibre 1 g; Cholesterol 355 mg; 1430 kJ (340 Cal)

Use scissors to cut the banana leaves into squares of approximately 18 cm (7 inches).

Enclose the filling and secure the parcel with a bamboo skewer.

Lime steamed chicken

PREPARATION TIME: 15 MINUTES I TOTAL COOKING TIME: 15 MINUTES I SERVES 4

2 limes, thinly sliced, plus extra, to serve
4 boneless, skinless chicken breasts
500 g (1 lb 2 oz/1 bunch) bok choy (pak choy)
500 g (1 lb 2 oz/1 bunch) choy sum
1 teaspoon sesame oil
1 tablespoon peanut oil
125 ml (4 fl oz/½ cup) oyster sauce
80 ml (2½ fl oz/⅓ cup) lime juice

1   Line the base of a bamboo steamer with the lime slices and place the chicken on top. Season. Place over a wok with a little water in the base, cover and steam for 8–10 minutes, or until the chicken is cooked through. Cover the chicken and keep warm. Drain and dry the wok.

2   Wash and trim the greens. Heat the oils in the wok and cook the greens for 2–3 minutes, or until just wilted.

3   Mix together the oyster sauce and lime juice and pour over the greens. Serve the chicken on top of the greens with some extra lime slices.

NOTE: *The Asian green vegetables used in this recipe, bok choy and choy sum, can be replaced by any green vegetables, such as broccoli, snow peas (mangetouts), or English spinach.*

NUTRITION PER SERVE
Protein 60 g; Fat 12 g; Carbohydrate 10 g; Dietary Fibre 4.5 g; Cholesterol 120 mg; 1665 kJ (398 Cal)

Line the base of the steamer with lime slices and then arrange the chicken on top.

Heat the oils in a wok and stir-fry the Asian greens until they are just wilted.

Mix together the oyster sauce and lime juice and pour over the greens.

Steamed trout with ginger and coriander

PREPARATION TIME: 20 MINUTES | TOTAL COOKING TIME: 30 MINUTES | SERVES 2

2 whole rainbow trout, cleaned and scaled
2 limes, thinly sliced
5 cm (2 inch) piece of fresh ginger, cut into
    matchsticks
50 g (2¼ oz/¼ cup) caster (superfine) sugar
60 ml (2 fl oz/¼ cup) lime juice
zest of 1 lime, cut into thin strips
1 large handful coriander (cilantro) leaves

1 Preheat the oven to 180°C (350°F/Gas 4). Fill the fish cavities with the lime slices and some of the ginger, then place the fish on a large piece of lightly greased foil. Wrap the fish and bake on a baking tray for 20–30 minutes, or until the flesh flakes easily when tested with a fork.

2 While the fish is cooking, combine the sugar and lime juice with 250 ml (9 fl oz/1 cup) water in a small saucepan and stir without boiling until the sugar dissolves. Bring to the boil, reduce the heat and simmer for 10 minutes, or until syrupy. Stir in the remaining ginger and lime strips. Put the fish on a plate. Top with coriander leaves and pour the hot syrup over it.

NUTRITION PER SERVE
Protein 50 g; Fat 10 g; Carbohydrate 30 g; Dietary Fibre 1 g; Cholesterol 120 mg; 1715 kJ (410 Cal)

Peel the piece of fresh ginger and cut it into fine, short matchsticks.

Fill the cavities of the trout with the lime slices and some of the ginger.

Simmer the sugar in the lime juice and water to make hot syrup.

Lemongrass and ginger chicken with Asian greens

PREPARATION TIME: 25 MINUTES | TOTAL COOKING TIME: 40 MINUTES | SERVES 4

200 g (7 oz) fresh egg noodles
4 boneless, skinless chicken breasts
2 lemongrass stems, white part only
5 cm (2 inch) piece fresh ginger, cut
   into matchsticks
1 lime, thinly sliced
500 ml (17 fl oz/2 cups) chicken stock
350 g (12 oz/1 bunch) choy sum, cut into
   10 cm (4 inch) lengths
800 g (1 lb 12 oz) Chinese broccoli, cut into
   10 cm (4 inch) lengths
60 ml (2 fl oz/¼ cup) kecap manis
   (see NOTE, page 37)
60 ml (2 fl oz/¼ cup) soy sauce
1 teaspoon sesame oil
sesame seeds, toasted, to garnish

1 Cook the egg noodles in a saucepan of boiling water for 5 minutes, then drain and keep warm.

2 Slice each chicken breast fillet horizontally to give 8 thin flat fillets.

3 Cut the lemongrass into lengths that are about 5 cm (2 inches) longer than the chicken fillets, then cut in half lengthways. Place one piece of lemongrass onto one half of each chicken breast, top with some ginger and lime slices, then top with the other half of the fillet.

4 Pour the stock into a wok and bring to a simmer. Place two of the chicken breasts in a paper-lined bamboo steamer. Place the steamer over the wok and steam over the simmering stock for 12–15 minutes, or until the chicken is tender. Remove the chicken from the steamer, cover and keep warm. Repeat with the other breasts.

5 Steam the greens in the same way for 3 minutes, or until tender. Bring the stock in the wok to the boil.

6 Whisk together the kecap manis, soy sauce and sesame oil.

7 Divide the noodles among four serving plates and ladle the boiling stock over them. Top with chicken and Asian greens and drizzle with the sauce. Sprinkle with toasted sesame seeds.

NUTRITION PER SERVE
Protein 65 g; Fat 7.5 g; Carbohydrate 37 g; Dietary Fibre 9 g; Cholesterol 119 mg; 2045 kJ (488 Cal)

Cut each chicken breast in half horizontally through the middle.

Top the bottom half of each breast with lemongrass, ginger and lime.

Steam the lemongrass chicken breasts until cooked and tender.

Hoisin barbecued chicken

PREPARATION TIME: 10 MINUTES + AT LEAST 2 HOURS MARINATING | TOTAL COOKING TIME: 25 MINUTES | SERVES 4–6

2 garlic cloves, finely chopped
60 ml (2 fl oz/¼ cup) hoisin sauce
3 teaspoons light soy sauce
3 teaspoons honey
1 teaspoon sesame oil
2 tablespoons tomato sauce (ketchup) or sweet chilli sauce
2 spring onions (scallions), finely sliced
1.5 kg (3 lb 5 oz) chicken wings

1 To make the marinade, mix together the garlic, hoisin sauce, soy sauce, honey, sesame oil, tomato sauce and spring onion. Pour over the chicken wings, cover and marinate in the refrigerator for at least 2 hours.

2 Cook the chicken on a chargrill pan or barbecue grill plate, turning once, for 20–25 minutes, or until cooked and golden brown. Baste with the marinade during cooking. Heat any remaining marinade in a pan until boiling and serve as a sauce.

NOTE: *The chicken can also be baked in a 180°C (350°F/Gas 4) oven for 30 minutes. Turn halfway through cooking.*

NUTRITION PER SERVE (6)
Protein 26 g; Fat 8.5 g; Carbohydrate 9 g; Dietary Fibre 1.5 g; Cholesterol 111 mg; 916 kJ (219 Cal)

Mix together the garlic, hoisin and soy sauces, honey, sesame oil, tomato sauce and spring onion.

Pour the marinade over the chicken wings and leave in the refrigerator for at least 2 hours.

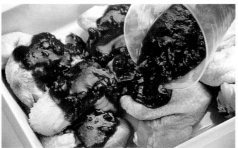

Cook the chicken wings on a chargrill pan or barbecue grill plate.

Indian spiced lamb

PREPARATION TIME: 15 MINUTES + 30 MINUTES MARINATING | TOTAL COOKING TIME: 20 MINUTES | SERVES 4–6

3 tablespoons oil
2 tablespoons madras curry powder,
   or to taste
4 lamb fillets
1 tablespoon brinjal pickle (see NOTES)
250 g (9 oz/1 cup) Greek-style yoghurt
350 g (12 oz) couscous
½ red capsicum (pepper), diced
4 spring onions (scallions), sliced

1 Mix together 2 tablespoons oil and the curry powder. Place the lamb in a non-metallic dish and brush the curry oil over it. Cover and marinate for 30 minutes. Preheat the oven to 180°C (350°F/Gas 4).

2 Place the brinjal pickle and yoghurt in a bowl and mix together well. Add 2 tablespoons water and set aside. Heat the remaining oil in a frying pan, add the lamb and cook for 2–3 minutes on each side to seal. Transfer to an ovenproof dish and cook in the oven for 10–12 minutes. Remove from the oven and rest, covered, for 5 minutes, then carve into slices.

3 Meanwhile, place the couscous in a bowl. Season with salt and cover with 455 ml (16 fl oz) boiling water. Leave for 5 minutes, or until all the liquid has been absorbed. Fluff the couscous with a fork to separate the grains. Cool, then add the capsicum, spring onion and half the yoghurt mixture. Serve the lamb slices on a bed of couscous. Drizzle the remaining yoghurt mixture over the top.

NOTES: *Brinjal pickle is made from eggplant (aubergine) and is widely available. If you can't find it, try mango chutney.*

With the couscous you can use orange juice instead of water, and nuts and sultanas (golden raisins) instead of capsicums and onions.

NUTRITION PER SERVE (6)
Protein 30 g; Fat 16 g; Carbohydrate 45 g; Dietary Fibre 3.5 g; Cholesterol 73 mg; 1881 kJ (450 Cal)

Put the lamb in a non-metallic dish and brush with the curry oil.

Mix together the brinjal pickle and yoghurt with a little water.

Steamed chicken with soy mushroom sauce

PREPARATION TIME: 10 MINUTES + 20 MINUTES SOAKING + AT LEAST 1 HOUR MARINATING I TOTAL COOKING TIME: 20 MINUTES I SERVES 4

10–15 g (¼–½ oz) dried Chinese mushrooms

2 tablespoons light soy sauce

2 tablespoons rice wine

½ teaspoon sesame oil

1 tablespoon finely sliced fresh ginger

4 boneless, skinless chicken breasts

450 g (1 lb) bok choy (pak choy), ends removed and cut lengthways into quarters

125 ml (4 fl oz/½ cup) chicken stock

1 tablespoon cornflour (cornstarch)

NUTRITION PER SERVE
Protein 46 g; Fat 6 g; Carbohydrate 5 g; Dietary Fibre 2 g; Cholesterol 95 mg; 1085 kJ (260 Cal)

1 Soak the dried mushrooms in 60 ml (2 fl oz/¼ cup) boiling water for 20 minutes. Drain and reserve the liquid. Discard the tough stalks and slice the caps thinly.

2 Combine the soy sauce, rice wine, sesame oil and ginger in a non-metallic dish. Add the chicken and turn to coat. Cover and marinate for at least 1 hour.

3 Line a bamboo steamer with baking paper. Place the chicken on top, reserving the marinade. Bring water to the boil in a wok, then place the steamer over the wok. Cover and steam the chicken for 6 minutes, then turn over and steam for a further 6 minutes. Place the bok choy on top of the chicken and steam for 2–3 minutes.

4 Meanwhile, place the reserved marinade, mushrooms and their soaking liquid in a small saucepan and bring to the boil. Add enough stock to the cornflour in a small bowl to make a smooth paste. Add the cornflour paste and remaining stock to the pan and stir for 2 minutes over medium heat, or until the sauce thickens.

5 Place some bok choy and a chicken breast on each plate, then pour on the sauce to serve.

Turn the chicken breasts until they are well coated in the marinade.

Place the lengths of bok choy in the bamboo steamer on top of the chicken.

Stir the marinating liquid and chicken stock mixture until the sauce thickens.

Japanese-style salmon parcels

PREPARATION TIME: *40* MINUTES I TOTAL COOKING TIME: *15* MINUTES I SERVES *4*

2 teaspoons sesame seeds
4 x 150 g (5½ oz) salmon cutlets or steaks
2.5 cm (1 inch) piece fresh ginger
2 celery stalks
4 spring onions (scallions)
3 tablespoons mirin (see NOTE)
2 tablespoons tamari
¼ teaspoon dashi granules

1 Cut baking paper into four squares large enough to wrap the salmon steaks. Preheat the oven to 230°C (450°F/Gas 8). Lightly toast the sesame seeds under a grill (broiler) or in the oven for a few minutes.

2 Wash the salmon and dry with paper towels. Place a salmon cutlet in the centre of each paper square.

3 Cut the ginger into paper-thin slices. Slice the celery and spring onions into short lengths, then lengthways into fine strips. Arrange a bundle of the prepared strips and several slices of ginger on each salmon steak.

4 Combine the mirin, tamari and dashi granules in a small saucepan. Heat gently until the granules dissolve. Drizzle over each parcel, sprinkle with sesame seeds and carefully wrap the salmon, folding in the sides to seal in all the juices. Arrange the parcels on a baking tray and cook for about 12 minutes, or until tender. (The paper will puff up when the fish is cooked.) Do not overcook or the salmon will dry out. Serve immediately, as standing time can spoil the fish.

NOTE: *Mirin, tamari and dashi are all available from Japanese food stores.*

Arrange celery and spring onion strips on the fish and top with ginger slices.

Wrap the salmon in baking paper, folding the sides in to seal the juices.

NUTRITION PER SERVE
Protein 20 g; Fat 14 g; Carbohydrate 0 g; Dietary Fibre 0.5 g; Cholesterol 85 mg; 935 kJ (225 Cal)

Crumbed fish with wasabi cream

PREPARATION TIME: 25 MINUTES + 15 MINUTES REFRIGERATION | TOTAL COOKING TIME: 20 MINUTES | SERVES 4

50 g (2¼ oz/¾ cup) fresh breadcrumbs
25 g (1 oz/¾ cup) cornflakes
1 sheet nori (dried seaweed), roughly torn
¼ teaspoon paprika
4 x 150 g (5½ oz) firm white fish fillets
plain (all-purpose) flour, for dusting
1 egg white
1 tablespoon skim milk
1 spring onion (scallion), thinly sliced

WASABI CREAM
125 g (4¼ oz/½ cup) low-fat plain yoghurt
1 teaspoon wasabi (see NOTE)
1 tablespoon mayonnaise
1 teaspoon lime juice

1 Preheat the oven to 180°C (350°F/ Gas 4). Combine the breadcrumbs, cornflakes, nori and paprika in a food processor and mix until the nori is finely chopped.

2 Dust the fish lightly with plain flour, dip into the combined egg white and milk, then into the breadcrumb mixture. Press the crumb mixture on firmly, then refrigerate for 15 minutes.

3 Line a baking tray with non-stick baking paper and put the fish on the paper. Bake for 15–20 minutes, or until the fish flakes easily when tested.

4 To make the wasabi cream, mix together all the ingredients. Serve a spoonful on top of the fish and sprinkle with spring onion.

NOTE: *Wasabi paste (a pungent paste, also known as Japanese horseradish) and nori (sheets of paper-thin dried seaweed) are both available from Japanese food stores.*

NUTRITION PER SERVE
Protein 35 g; Fat 6 g; Carbohydrate 25 g; Dietary Fibre 1 g; Cholesterol 105 mg; 1270 kJ (305 Cal)

Process the breadcrumbs, cornflakes, nori and paprika together.

Dust the fish with flour, dip in the egg and milk, then press in the breadcrumb mixture.

Curries

Balti chicken

PREPARATION TIME: 25 MINUTES | TOTAL COOKING TIME: 1 HOUR | SERVES 6

1 kg (2 lb 4 oz) boneless, skinless
    chicken thighs
80 ml (2½ fl oz/⅓ cup) oil
1 large red onion, finely chopped
4–5 garlic cloves, finely chopped
1 tablespoon grated fresh ginger
2 teaspoons ground cumin
2 teaspoons ground coriander
1 teaspoon ground turmeric
½ teaspoon chilli powder
425 g (15 oz) tin chopped tomatoes
1 green capsicum (pepper), seeded and diced
1–2 small green chillies, seeded and
    finely chopped
4 tablespoons chopped coriander (cilantro)
2 spring onions (scallions), chopped,
    to garnish

1   Remove any excess fat or sinew from the chicken thighs and cut into four or five even-sized pieces.

2   Heat a large wok over high heat, add the oil and swirl to coat the side. Add the onion and stir-fry over medium heat for 5 minutes, or until softened but not browned. Add the garlic and ginger and stir-fry for 3 more minutes.

3   Add the spices, 1 teaspoon salt and 60 ml (2 fl oz/¼ cup) water. Increase the heat to high and stir-fry for 2 minutes, or until the mixture has thickened. Take care not to burn.

4   Add the tomato and 250 ml (9 fl oz/1 cup) water and cook, stirring often, for a further 10 minutes, or until the mixture is thick and pulpy and the oil comes to the surface.

5   Add the chicken to the pan, reduce the heat and simmer, stirring often, for 15 minutes. Add the capsicum and chilli and simmer for a further 25 minutes, or until the chicken is tender. Add a little water if the mixture is too thick. Stir in the coriander and garnish with the spring onion.

NOTE: *This curry is traditionally cooked in a Karahi pan—a wok is a good substitute.*

NUTRITION PER SERVE
Protein 40 g; Fat 17 g; Carbohydrate 5 g; Dietary
Fibre 2 g; Cholesterol 83 mg; 1370 kJ (327 Cal)

Remove any excess fat or sinew from the chicken, then cut into even-sized pieces.

Add the spices, salt and water to the wok and cook until thickened.

Cook, stirring, until the curry thickens and the oil comes to the surface.

Cauliflower curry

PREPARATION TIME: 20 MINUTES + 30 MINUTES MARINATING | TOTAL COOKING TIME: 20 MINUTES | SERVES 6

MARINADE
1 large onion, roughly chopped
1 teaspoon grated fresh ginger
2 garlic cloves, crushed
3 green chillies, chopped
60 g (2¼ oz/¼ cup) plain yoghurt

1 cauliflower, divided into florets
oil, for deep-frying

CURRY SAUCE
2 tablespoons ghee
1 onion, finely chopped
2 tablespoons tomato paste
   (concentrated purée)
2 tablespoons pouring (whipping) cream
1 teaspoon chilli powder
1½ tablespoons garam masala

1 To make the marinade, place all the ingredients in a food processor and mix until smooth. Place the marinade in a bowl, add the cauliflower, toss to coat and leave for 30 minutes.

2 Fill a deep heavy-based saucepan one-third full of oil and heat to 160°C (315°F), or until a cube of bread dropped into the oil browns in 30–35 seconds. Cook the cauliflower in batches for 30 seconds until golden brown all over. Drain on paper towels.

3 Heat the ghee in a frying pan, add the onion and cook for 4–5 minutes, or until soft. Add the tomato paste, cream, chilli powder, garam masala, 375 ml (13 fl oz/1½ cups) water and salt to taste. Cook, stirring constantly, over medium heat for 3 minutes.

4 Add the cauliflower and cook for 7 minutes, adding a little water if the sauce becomes dry.

Mix all the marinade ingredients in a food processor until smooth.

Heat the oil until a cube of bread dropped into the pan browns in 30–35 seconds.

NUTRITION PER SERVE
Protein 2.5 g; Fat 9 g; Carbohydrate 4.5 g; Dietary Fibre 2 g; Cholesterol 27 mg; 458 kJ (110 Cal)

Beef rendang

PREPARATION TIME: 20 MINUTES | TOTAL COOKING TIME: 2 HOURS 30 MINUTES | SERVES 6

onions, roughly chopped
garlic cloves, crushed
00 ml (14 fl oz) coconut milk
teaspoons ground coriander seeds
½ teaspoon ground fennel seeds
teaspoons ground cumin seeds
4 teaspoon ground cloves
.5 kg (3 lb 5 oz) chuck steak, cubed
-6 small red chillies, chopped
tablespoon lemon juice
lemongrass stem, white part only, bruised,
    cut lengthways
teaspoons grated palm sugar (jaggery) or soft
    brown sugar

Mix the onion and garlic in a food processor until smooth, adding water, if necessary.

Put the coconut milk in a large saucepan and bring to the boil. Reduce the heat to medium and cook, stirring occasionally, for 15 minutes, or until reduced by half and the oil has separated. Do not allow to brown.

Add the coriander, fennel, cumin and cloves to the pan and stir for 1 minute. Add the meat and cook for 2 minutes, or until it changes colour. Add the onion mixture, chilli, lemon juice, lemongrass and sugar. Cook, covered, over medium heat for 2 hours, or until the liquid has reduced and the mixture has thickened. Stir frequently to prevent sticking.

Uncover and cook until the oil from the coconut milk begins to emerge again, giving colour and flavour. Be careful not to burn. The curry is cooked when it is brown and dry.

NUTRITION PER SERVE
Protein 53 g; Fat 20 g; Carbohydrate 6 g; Dietary Fibre 1.5 g; Cholesterol 168 mg; 1775 kJ (424 Cal)

Mix the onion and garlic in a food processor until smooth, adding water if necessary.

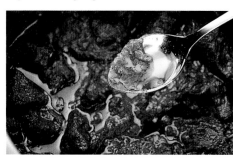
Continue to cook until the oil from the coconut mix begins to emerge again.

Madras beef curry

PREPARATION TIME: 20 MINUTES | TOTAL COOKING TIME: 1 HOUR 45 MINUTES | SERVES 6

1 tablespoon vegetable oil
2 onions, finely chopped
3 garlic cloves, finely chopped
1 tablespoon grated fresh ginger
4 tablespoons madras curry paste
1 kg (2 lb 4 oz) chuck steak, diced
60 g (2¼ oz/¼ cup) tomato paste
    (concentrated purée)
250 ml (9 fl oz/1 cup) beef stock
6 new potatoes, halved
155 g (5½ oz/1 cup) frozen peas

NUTRITION PER SERVE
Protein 40 g; Fat 13 g; Carbohydrate 15 g; Dietary
Fibre 5.5 g; Cholesterol 112 mg; 1410 kJ (335 Cal)

1 Preheat the oven to 180°C (350°F/Gas 4). Heat the oil in a large heavy-based 3 litre (105 fl oz/12 cup) flameproof casserole. Cook the onion over medium heat for 4–5 minutes. Add the garlic and ginger and cook, stirring, for 5 minutes, or until the onion is lightly golden, taking care not to burn it.

2 Add the curry paste and cook, stirring, for 2 minutes, or until fragrant. Increase the heat to high, add the meat and stir constantly for 2–3 minutes, or until the meat is well coated. Add the tomato paste and stock and stir well.

3 Bake, covered, for 50 minutes, stirring 2–3 times during cooking, and add a little water if necessary. Reduce the oven to 160°C (315°F/Gas 2–3). Add the potato and cook for 30 minutes, then add the peas and cook for another 10 minutes, or until the potato is tender.

Fry the onion, garlic and ginger until the onion is lightly golden.

Stir the cubes of steak into the curry paste until well coated.

Add the potato halves and cook for 30 minutes.

Beef and pineapple curry

PREPARATION TIME: 10 MINUTES | TOTAL COOKING TIME: 12 MINUTES | SERVES 4

2 tablespoons peanut oil

500 g (1 lb 2 oz) rump steak, thinly sliced
across the grain

2 tablespoons penang curry paste

2 onions, cut into thin wedges

2 garlic cloves, crushed

500 ml (17 fl oz/2 cups) tin coconut milk

8 makrut (kaffir lime) leaves

320 g (11¼ oz/2 cups) chopped
fresh pineapple

2 teaspoons soft brown sugar

2 tablespoons lime juice

1 tablespoon fish sauce

3 tablespoons chopped coriander (cilantro)
leaves

1   Heat a wok over high heat, add half the oil
and swirl to coat the sides. Add the beef in
batches and stir-fry for 2 minutes, or until
browned. Remove.

2   Heat the remaining oil in the wok over high
heat, add the curry paste and cook for 1 minute,
or until fragrant. Add the onion and garlic and
cook for 1–2 minutes, or until the onion is soft.

3   Return the beef to the wok, add the coconut
milk, makrut leaves and pineapple and bring to
the boil, then reduce the heat and simmer for
5 minutes, or until the beef is just cooked. Stir in
the remaining ingredients just before serving.

Stir-fry the beef in batches over high heat until it is
all browned.

Add the onion and garlic to the wok and cook until
the onion is soft.

NUTRITION PER SERVE
Protein 47 g; Fat 53 g; Carbohydrate 23 g; Dietary
Fibre 7 g; Cholesterol 118 mg; 3137 kJ (749 Cal)

Kashmir lamb with spinach

PREPARATION TIME: 20 MINUTES | TOTAL COOKING TIME: 1 HOUR 30 MINUTES | SERVES 4

2 tablespoons oil
750 g (1 lb 10 oz) diced leg of lamb
2 large onions, chopped
3 garlic cloves, crushed
5 cm (2 inch) piece fresh ginger, grated
2 teaspoons ground cumin
2 teaspoons ground coriander
2 teaspoons turmeric
¼ teaspoon ground cardamom
¼ teaspoon ground cloves
3 bay leaves
375 ml (13 fl oz/1½ cups) chicken stock
125 ml (4 fl oz/½ cup) pouring
  (whipping) cream
2 bunches English spinach leaves, washed
  and chopped

1 Heat the oil in a heavy-based pan and brown the lamb in batches. Remove from the pan. Add the onion, garlic and ginger and cook for 3 minutes, stirring regularly. Add the cumin, coriander, turmeric, cardamom and cloves and cook, stirring, for 1–2 minutes, or until fragrant. Return the lamb to the pan with any juices. Add the bay leaves and stock.

2 Bring to the boil and then reduce the heat, stir well, cover and simmer for 35 minutes. Add the cream and cook, covered, for a further 20 minutes or until the lamb is very tender.

3 Add the spinach and cook until it has softened. Season to taste before serving.

STORAGE: *Curry is best cooked a day in advance and refrigerated. Do not add the spinach until reheating.*

NUTRITION PER SERVE
Protein 45 g; Fat 25 g; Carbohydrate 3 g; Dietary Fibre 2 g; Cholesterol 165 mg; 1820 kJ (435 Cal)

Return the browned lamb to the pan and add the bay leaves.

Stir in the cream and simmer, covered, until the lamb is very tender.

Bombay lamb curry

PREPARATION TIME: 25 MINUTES I TOTAL COOKING TIME: 1 HOUR 25 MINUTES I SERVES 4–6

1.5 kg (3 lb 5 oz) leg of lamb, boned
(ask your butcher to do this)
2 tablespoons ghee or oil
2 onions, finely chopped
2 garlic cloves, crushed
2 small green chillies, finely chopped
5 cm (2 inch) piece fresh ginger, grated
1½ teaspoons turmeric
2 teaspoons ground cumin
3 teaspoons ground coriander
½–1 teaspoon chilli powder
425 g (15 oz) tin chopped tomatoes
2 tablespoons coconut cream

1   Cut the meat into cubes, removing any skin and fat. You will have about 1 kg (2 lb 4 oz) meat remaining. Heat the ghee or oil in a large heavy-based frying pan. Add the onion and cook, stirring frequently, over medium–high heat for 10 minutes until golden brown. Add the garlic, chilli and ginger and stir for a further 2 minutes, taking care not to burn them.

2   Mix together the turmeric, cumin, coriander and chilli powder. Stir to a smooth paste with 2 tablespoons water and add to the frying pan. Stir for 2 minutes, taking care not to burn.

3   Add the meat a handful at a time, stirring well to coat with spices. It is important to make sure all the meat is well-coated and browned.

4   Add 1–1½ teaspoons salt to taste and stir in the tomatoes. Bring to the boil, cover and reduce the heat to low. Simmer for 30 minutes and then stir in the coconut cream. Simmer for another 30 minutes, or until the lamb is tender.

STORAGE: *Keep covered and refrigerated for up to 3 days. The flavour of curry improves if kept for at least a day.*

NUTRITION PER SERVE (6)
Protein 58 g; Fat 13 g; Carbohydrate 5 g; Dietary Fibre 1.5 g; Cholesterol 165 mg; 1565 kJ (375 Cal)

Cut the meat into bite-sized chunks, removing any fat as you cut.

Once the onion is golden brown, stir in the garlic, chilli and ginger.

Blend the ground spices to a smooth paste with a little water.

Thai red vegetable curry

PREPARATION TIME: 10 MINUTES I TOTAL COOKING TIME: 25 MINUTES I SERVES 4

1 tablespoon peanut oil
250 g (9 oz) broccoli florets, quartered
250 g (9 oz) cauliflower florets, quartered
500 g (1 lb 2 oz) orange sweet potato, cut into
    even-size chunks
2 tablespoons Thai red curry paste
500 ml (17 fl oz/2 cups) coconut milk
1 tablespoon lime juice
1 tablespoon fish sauce, optional
3 tablespoons chopped coriander (cilantro)

1 Heat a wok over high heat, add the oil and swirl to coat the side. Add the broccoli, cauliflower and sweet potato in batches and stir-fry for 3 minutes. Add 60 ml (2 fl oz/¼ cup) water and cover. Reduce the heat to low for 8–10 minutes to steam the vegetables.

2 Add the curry paste and cook over medium heat for 30 seconds, or until fragrant. Stir in the coconut milk and simmer for 8 minutes, or until slightly thickened. Add the lime juice, fish sauce and coriander.

Steam the vegetables in the wok until they are just cooked but still crunchy.

Add the coconut milk to the wok and simmer until slightly thickened.

NUTRITION PER SERVE
Protein 22 g; Fat 63 g; Carbohydrate 40 g; Dietary
Fibre 18 g; Cholesterol 0.5 mg; 3434 kJ (820 Cal)

Thai green chicken curry

PREPARATION TIME: 40 MINUTES | TOTAL COOKING TIME: 30 MINUTES | SERVES 4–6

500 ml (17 fl oz/2 cups) coconut cream;
   do not shake the tin (see NOTE)
4 tablespoons Thai green curry paste
2 tablespoons grated palm sugar (jaggery)
2 tablespoons fish sauce
4 makrut (kaffir lime) leaves, finely shredded
1 kg (2 lb 4 oz) boneless, skinless chicken
   thighs or breasts, cut into thick strips
200 g (7 oz) tinned bamboo shoots, cut into
   thick strips
100 g (3½ oz) snake (yard-long) beans,
   cut into short lengths
1 handful Thai basil leaves, plus extra,
   to garnish

1   Open the tin of coconut cream and lift off
the thick cream from the top; you should have
about 125 ml (4 fl oz/½ cup). Put in a wok or
saucepan and bring to the boil. Add the curry
paste, then reduce the heat and simmer for
15 minutes, or until fragrant and the oil starts to
separate from the cream. Add the palm sugar,
fish sauce and makrut leaves.

2   Stir in the remaining coconut cream and the
chicken, bamboo shoots and beans and simmer
for 15 minutes, or until the chicken is tender. Stir
in the Thai basil just before serving. Garnish
with the extra leaves.

NOTE: *Do not shake the tin, because good-
quality coconut cream has a layer of very thick
cream at the top. This has a higher fat content,
which causes it to split or separate more readily
than the rest of the coconut cream or milk.*

Lift off the thick cream from the top of the tin of coconut cream.

Simmer the coconut cream and curry paste until the oil separates.

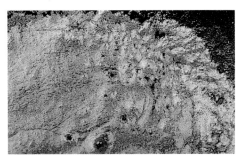

NUTRITION PER SERVE (6)
Protein 40 g; Fat 22 g; Carbohydrate 11 g; Dietary
Fibre 2 g; Cholesterol 85 mg; 1698 kJ (405 Cal)

Malaysian chicken kapitan

PREPARATION TIME: 35 MINUTES | TOTAL COOKING TIME: 1 HOUR 20 MINUTES | SERVES 4–6

1 teaspoon small dried shrimp
80 ml (2½ fl oz/⅓ cup) oil
6–8 red chillies, seeded and finely chopped
4 garlic cloves, finely chopped
3 lemongrass stems, white part only,
    finely chopped
2 teaspoons ground turmeric
10 candlenuts
2 large onions, chopped
250 ml (9 fl oz/1 cup) coconut milk
1.5 kg (3 lb 5 oz) chicken, cut into 8 pieces
125 ml (4 fl oz/½ cup) coconut cream
2 tablespoons lime juice
makrut (kaffir lime) leaves, shredded,
    to garnish

1 Put the dried shrimp in a frying pan and dry-fry over low heat, shaking the pan regularly, for 3 minutes, or until the shrimp are dark orange and are giving off a strong aroma. Transfer to a mortar and pestle and pound until finely ground. Alternatively, process in a food processor.

2 Mix half the oil, the chilli, garlic, lemongrass, turmeric and candlenuts in a food processor until very finely chopped, regularly scraping down the bowl with a rubber spatula.

3 Heat the remaining oil in a wok or frying pan, add the onion and ¼ teaspoon salt and cook, stirring regularly, over low heat for 8 minutes, or until golden. Add the spice mixture and ground shrimp and stir for 5 minutes. If the mixture begins to stick to the bottom of the pan, add 2 tablespoons coconut milk. It is important to cook the mixture thoroughly to develop the flavours.

4 Add the chicken to the wok and cook, stirring, for 5 minutes, or until beginning to brown. Stir in the remaining coconut milk and 250 ml (9 fl oz/1 cup) water and bring to the boil. Reduce the heat and simmer for 50 minutes, or until the chicken is cooked and the sauce has thickened slightly. Add the coconut cream and bring the mixture back to the boil, stirring constantly. Add the lime juice before serving. Garnish with the makrut leaves.

NUTRITION PER SERVE (6)
Protein 58 g; Fat 30 g; Carbohydrate 4 g; Dietary Fibre 2 g; Cholesterol 125 mg; 2211 kJ (528 Cal)

Dry-fry the shrimp over low heat until they turn dark orange.

Place the shrimp in a mortar and pestle and pound until finely ground.

Simmer until the chicken is cooked and the sauce has thickened slightly.

Pork vindaloo

PREPARATION TIME: 20 MINUTES | TOTAL COOKING TIME: 2 HOURS | SERVES 4

60 ml (2 fl oz/¼ cup) oil
1 kg (2 lb 4 oz) pork fillets, cubed
2 onions, finely chopped
4 garlic cloves, finely chopped
1 tablespoon finely chopped fresh ginger
1 tablespoon garam masala
2 teaspoons brown mustard seeds
4 tablespoons vindaloo paste

1   Heat the oil in a frying pan, add the meat in small batches and brown over medium heat for 5–7 minutes. Remove all the meat from the pan.

2   Add the onion, garlic, ginger, garam masala and mustard seeds to the pan and cook, stirring, for 5 minutes, or until the onion is soft.

3   Return all the meat to the pan, add the vindaloo paste and cook, stirring, for 2 minutes. Add 625 ml (21½ fl oz/2½ cups) water and bring to the boil. Reduce the heat and simmer, covered, for 1½ hours, or until the meat is tender.

NUTRITION PER SERVE
Protein 58 g; Fat 20 g; Carbohydrate 4 g; Dietary Fibre 2 g; Cholesterol 125 mg; 1806 kJ (430 Cal)

Trim the pork of any excess fat or sinew and cut into cubes.

Cook the pork in small batches over medium heat until browned.

Add the vindaloo paste and cook the curry until the meat is tender.

Malaysian nonya chicken curry

PREPARATION TIME: 20 MINUTES | TOTAL COOKING TIME: 35 MINUTES | SERVES 4

CURRY PASTE

red onions, chopped
small red chillies, seeded and sliced
garlic cloves, sliced
lemongrass stems, white part only, sliced
cm (2 inch) piece galangal, sliced
makrut (kaffir lime) leaves, roughly chopped
teaspoon ground turmeric
teaspoon shrimp paste, dry-roasted

tablespoons oil
50 g (1 lb 10 oz) boneless, skinless chicken
   thighs, cut into bite-sized pieces
00 ml (14 fl oz) coconut milk
tablespoons tamarind purée
tablespoon fish sauce

To make the curry paste, place all the ingredients in a food processor or blender and mix to a thick paste.

Heat a wok or large saucepan over high heat, add the oil and swirl to coat the side. Add the curry paste and cook, stirring occasionally, over ow heat for 8–10 minutes, or until fragrant. Add he chicken and stir-fry with the paste for 2–3 minutes.

Add the coconut milk, tamarind purée and fish sauce to the wok, and simmer, stirring occasionally, for 15–20 minutes, or until the chicken is tender.

Place the curry paste ingredients in a food processor and mix to a thick paste.

Trim the chicken of any excess fat or sinew and cut into bite-sized pieces.

NUTRITION PER SERVE
Protein 45 g; Fat 35 g; Carbohydrate 8 g; Dietary
Fibre 4 g; Cholesterol 94 mg; 2175 kJ (520 Cal)

Massaman beef curry

PREPARATION TIME: 30 MINUTES I TOTAL COOKING TIME: 1 HOUR 45 MINUTES I SERVES 4

1 tablespoon tamarind pulp

2 tablespoons oil

750 g (1 lb 10 oz) lean stewing beef, cubed

500 ml (17 fl oz/2 cups) coconut milk

4 cardamom pods, bruised

500 ml (17 fl oz/2 cups) coconut cream

2–3 tablespoons massaman curry paste

8 baby onions, peeled

8 new potatoes, peeled

2 tablespoons fish sauce

2 tablespoons palm sugar (jaggery)

90 g (3¼ oz/⅔ cup) unsalted peanuts, roasted
    and ground

coriander (cilantro) leaves, to garnish

NUTRITION PER SERVE
Protein 52 g; Fat 77 g; Carbohydrate 35 g; Dietary
Fibre 7.5 g; Cholesterol 115 mg; 4324 kJ (1033 Cal)

1   Place the tamarind pulp and 125 ml (4 fl oz/½ cup) boiling water in a bowl and set aside to cool. When cool, mash the pulp to dissolve in the water, then strain and reserve the liquid. Discard the pulp.

2   Heat the oil in a wok or a large saucepan and cook the beef in batches over high heat for 5 minutes, or until browned. Reduce the heat and add the coconut milk and cardamom, and simmer for 1 hour, or until the beef is tender. Remove and reserve the beef. Strain and reserve the cooking liquid, discarding the solids.

3   Heat the coconut cream in the wok and stir in the curry paste. Cook for 5 minutes, or until the oil starts to separate from the cream.

4   Add the baby onions, potatoes, fish sauce, palm sugar, peanuts, beef mixture, reserved cooking liquid and tamarind water, and simmer for 25–30 minutes. Garnish with coriander leaves to serve.

Mash the tamarind pulp with a fork, then strain and reserve the liquid.

Cook the beef in batches over high heat until it is all browned.

Cook the coconut cream and curry paste until the oil starts to separate from the cream.

Thai prawn curry

PREPARATION TIME: 30 MINUTES | TOTAL COOKING TIME: 10 MINUTES | SERVES 4

5 cm (2 inch) piece galangal
1 small onion, roughly chopped
3 garlic cloves
4 dried long red chillies
4 whole black peppercorns
2 tablespoons chopped lemongrass, white
    part only
1 tablespoon chopped coriander (cilantro)
    root
2 teaspoons grated lime zest
2 teaspoons cumin seeds
1 teaspoon sweet paprika
1 teaspoon ground coriander
3 tablespoons oil
1–2 tablespoons fish sauce
2 makrut (kaffir lime) leaves
500 ml (17 fl oz/2 cups) coconut cream
1 kg (2 lb 4 oz) raw prawns (shrimp), peeled
    and deveined

1 Peel the galangal and thinly slice. Mix the onion, garlic, chillies, peppercorns, lemongrass, coriander root, lime zest, cumin seeds, paprika, ground coriander, 2 tablespoons oil and ½ teaspoon salt in a food processor until a smooth paste forms.

2 Heat the remaining oil in a frying pan. Add half the curry paste and stir over medium heat for 2 minutes. (Left-over curry paste can be kept in the refrigerator for up to 2 weeks. It can also be frozen for up to 2 months.) Stir in the fish sauce, galangal, makrut leaves and coconut cream.

3 Add the prawns to the pan and simmer for 5 minutes, or until the prawns are cooked and the sauce has thickened slightly.

Peel the galangal and use a sharp knife to cut it into very thin slices.

Add half the curry paste to the pan and stir over medium heat for 2 minutes.

NUTRITION PER SERVE
Protein 42 g; Fat 40 g; Carbohydrate 9 g; Dietary
Fibre 4 g; Cholesterol 280 mg; 2310 kJ (550 Cal)

Malaysian fish curry

PREPARATION TIME: 25 MINUTES | TOTAL COOKING TIME: 25 MINUTES | SERVES 4

cm (2 inch) piece fresh ginger

–6 medium red chillies

onion, chopped

garlic cloves, chopped

lemongrass stems, white part only, sliced

teaspoons shrimp paste

0 ml (2 fl oz/¼ cup) oil

tablespoon fish curry powder (see NOTE)

50 ml (9 fl oz/1 cup) coconut milk

tablespoon tamarind concentrate

tablespoon kecap manis (see NOTE, page 37)

00 g (1 lb 2 oz) firm white skinless fish fillets, cut into cubes

ripe tomatoes, chopped

tablespoon lemon juice

Slice the ginger and mix in a small food processor with the chillies, onion, garlic, lemongrass and shrimp paste until roughly chopped. Add 2 tablespoons of the oil and process until a paste forms, regularly scraping the side of the bowl with a spatula.

Heat the remaining oil in a wok or deep, heavy-based frying pan and add the paste. Cook for 3–4 minutes over low heat, stirring constantly, until fragrant. Add the curry powder and stir for 2 minutes. Add the coconut milk, tamarind, kecap manis and 250 ml (9 fl oz/ cup) water. Bring to the boil, stirring occasionally, then reduce the heat and simmer or 10 minutes.

Add the fish, tomato and lemon juice. Season o taste, then simmer for 5 minutes, or until the ish is just cooked (it will flake easily).

NOTE: *Fish curry powder blend is available from peciality stores.*

NUTRITION PER SERVE
Protein 30 g; Fat 31 g; Carbohydrate 11 g; Dietary Fibre 4 g; Cholesterol 89 mg; 1810 kJ (430 Cal)

Add 2 tablespoons of oil to the chilli mixture and process to a paste.

Add the curry powder to the wok and stir for 2 minutes.

Lamb kofta curry

PREPARATION TIME: 25 MINUTES | TOTAL COOKING TIME: 35 MINUTES | SERVES 4

500 g (1 lb 2 oz) minced (ground) lean lamb
1 onion, finely chopped
1 garlic clove, finely chopped
1 teaspoon grated fresh ginger
1 small fresh chilli, finely chopped
1 teaspoon garam masala
1 teaspoon ground coriander
25 g (1 oz/¼ cup) ground almonds
2 tablespoons coriander (cilantro) leaves
plain yoghurt, to serve

SAUCE
2 teaspoons oil
1 onion, finely chopped
3 tablespoons korma curry paste
400 g (14 oz) tin chopped tomatoes
125 g (4½ oz/½ cup) low-fat yoghurt
1 teaspoon lemon juice

1   Combine the lamb, onion, garlic, ginger, chilli, garam masala, ground coriander, ground almonds and 1 teaspoon salt in a bowl. Shape into walnut-sized balls with your hands.

2   Heat a large non-stick frying pan and cook the koftas in batches until brown on both sides—they don't have to be cooked all the way through.

3   To make the sauce, heat the oil in a frying pan over low heat. Add the onion and cook for 6–8 minutes, or until soft and golden. Add the curry paste and cook until fragrant. Add the tomatoes and simmer for 5 minutes. Stir in the yoghurt, a tablespoon at a time, and then the lemon juice.

4   Put the koftas in the tomato sauce. Cook, covered, over low heat for 20 minutes. Garnish with the coriander leaves and serve with the yoghurt.

NUTRITION PER SERVE
Protein 32 g; Fat 23 g; Carbohydrate 10 g; Dietary Fibre 5 g; Cholesterol 88 mg; 1575 kJ (375 Cal)

Roll the lamb mixture into walnut-sized balls with your hands.

Add the chopped tomatoes and simmer for 5 minutes.

Add the koftas to the tomato sauce and cook over low heat for 20 minutes.

Butter chicken

PREPARATION TIME: 10 MINUTES I TOTAL COOKING TIME: 35 MINUTES I SERVES 4–6

2 tablespoons peanut oil

1 kg (2 lb 4 oz) boneless, skinless chicken thighs, quartered

60 g (2¼ oz) butter or ghee

2 teaspoons garam masala

2 teaspoons sweet paprika

2 teaspoons ground coriander

1 tablespoon finely chopped fresh ginger

¼ teaspoon chilli powder

1 cinnamon stick

6 cardamom pods, bruised

350 g (12 oz) tomato passata (puréed tomatoes)

1 tablespoon sugar

60 g (2¼ oz/¼ cup) plain yoghurt

125 ml (4 fl oz/½ cup) pouring (whipping) cream

1 tablespoon lemon juice

coriander (cilantro) leaves, to garnish

1 Heat a wok until very hot, add 1 tablespoon oil and swirl to coat. Add half the chicken thighs and stir-fry for 4 minutes, or until browned. Remove. Add extra oil, as needed, and cook the remaining chicken. Remove.

2 Reduce the heat, add the butter or ghee to the wok and melt. Add the garam masala, sweet paprika, ground coriander, ginger, chilli powder, cinnamon stick and cardamom pods and stir-fry for 1 minute, or until fragrant. Return the chicken to the wok and mix to coat in the spices.

3 Add the tomato passata and sugar, and simmer, stirring, for 15 minutes, or until the chicken is tender and the sauce has thickened.

4 Add the yoghurt, cream and juice and simmer for 5 minutes, or until the sauce has thickened slightly. Serve with rice or poppadoms and garnish with coriander leaves.

Stir-fry the chicken pieces in two batches until they are browned.

Simmer until the chicken is tender and the sauce has thickened.

NUTRITION PER SERVE (6)
Protein 40 g; Fat 28 g; Carbohydrate 6 g; Dietary Fibre 1 g; Cholesterol 140 mg; 1790 kJ (427 Cal)

Thai green fish curry

PREPARATION TIME: 15 MINUTES | TOTAL COOKING TIME: 15 MINUTES | SERVES 4

1 tablespoon peanut oil
1 onion, chopped
1½ tablespoons Thai green curry paste
375 ml (13 fl oz/1½ cups) coconut milk
750 g (1 lb 10 oz) boneless firm white fish
    fillets, cut into bite-sized pieces
3 makrut (kaffir lime) leaves
1 tablespoon fish sauce
2 teaspoons grated palm sugar (jaggery)
2 tablespoons lime juice
1 long green chilli, finely sliced

1 Heat a wok until very hot, add the oil and swirl to coat. Add the onion and stir-fry for 2 minutes, or until soft. Add the curry paste and stir-fry for 1–2 minutes, or until fragrant. Stir in the coconut milk and bring to the boil.

2 Add the fish and makrut leaves to the wok, reduce the heat and simmer, stirring occasionally, for 8–10 minutes, or until the fish is cooked through.

3 Stir in the fish sauce, palm sugar and lime juice. Scatter the chilli slices over the curry before serving.

NUTRITION PER SERVE
Protein 39 g; Fat 29 g; Carbohydrate 4.5 g; Dietary Fibre 1 g; Cholesterol 125 mg; 1820 kJ (435 Cal)

To prevent skin irritation, wear rubber gloves when slicing the chilli.

Heat the coconut milk to boiling point before adding the fish.

Gently simmer the fish pieces, stirring occasionally, until cooked through.

Chickpea curry

PREPARATION TIME: 10 MINUTES + OVERNIGHT SOAKING | TOTAL COOKING TIME: 1 HOUR 15 MINUTES | SERVES 6

220 g (7¾ oz/1 cup) dried chickpeas
2 tablespoons oil
2 onions, finely chopped
2 large ripe tomatoes, chopped
½ teaspoon ground coriander
1 teaspoon ground cumin
1 teaspoon chilli powder
¼ teaspoon ground turmeric
1 tablespoon channa (chole) masala
  (see NOTE)
1 tablespoon ghee or butter
1 small white onion, sliced, to garnish
mint and coriander (cilantro) leaves,
  to garnish

NUTRITION PER SERVE
Protein 8 g; Fat 11 g; Carbohydrate 17 g; Dietary
Fibre 6 g; Cholesterol 8.5 mg; 835 kJ (200 Cal)

1   Place the chickpeas in a bowl, cover with water and leave to soak overnight. Drain, rinse and place in a large saucepan. Cover with plenty of water and bring to the boil, then reduce the heat and simmer for 40 minutes, or until tender. Drain.

2   Heat the oil in a large saucepan, add the onion and cook over medium heat for 15 minutes, or until golden brown. Add the tomato, ground coriander and cumin, chilli powder, turmeric and channa (chole) masala. Add 500 ml (17 fl oz/2 cups) water and cook for 10 minutes, or until the tomato is soft. Add the chickpeas, season well with salt and cook for 7–10 minutes, or until the sauce thickens. Transfer to a serving dish. Place the ghee or butter on top and allow to melt before serving. Garnish with sliced onion and fresh mint and coriander leaves.

NOTE: *Channa (chole) masala is a spice blend specifically used in this dish. It is available at Indian grocery stores. Garam masala can be used as a substitute if unavailable, but this will alter the final flavour.*

Cook the onion in a large saucepan over medium heat until golden brown.

Add the chickpeas to the curry and cook until the sauce thickens.

Beef and spinach curry

PREPARATION TIME: 30 MINUTES | TOTAL COOKING TIME: 1 HOUR 15 MINUTES | SERVES 4

2 tablespoons oil
1 onion, finely chopped
2 garlic cloves, finely chopped
2 teaspoons ground cumin
2 teaspoons ground coriander
2 teaspoons paprika
1 teaspoon garam masala
1 teaspoon turmeric
½ teaspoon finely chopped red chilli
1 teaspoon finely chopped green chilli
2 teaspoons grated fresh ginger
500 g (1 lb 2 oz) lean minced (ground) beef
　　or lamb
1 tomato, chopped
250 ml (9 fl oz/1 cup) beef stock or water
500 g (1 lb 2 oz) English spinach, chopped
200 g (7 oz) plain yoghurt

1 Heat 1 tablespoon of the oil in a large saucepan and cook the onion over medium heat until golden brown. Add the garlic, cumin, coriander, paprika, garam masala, turmeric, red and green chilli and the grated ginger and stir for 1 minute. Remove and set aside.

2 Heat the remaining oil in the pan and brown the meat over high heat, breaking up any lumps with a fork or wooden spoon. Return the onion mixture to the pan and add the tomato and stock or water.

3 Bring the mixture to the boil and then reduce the heat and simmer for about 1 hour. Season with salt, to taste. Meanwhile, cook the spinach briefly. Just before serving, add the spinach to the mixture and stir in the yoghurt.

NOTE: *If possible, make the meat mixture in advance and refrigerate overnight for the flavours to develop.*

Finely chop the chillies. Wear rubber gloves to prevent skin irritation.

Add the garlic, spices, red and green chilli and ginger to the pan and stir.

NUTRITION PER SERVE
Protein 35 g; Fat 15 g; Carbohydrate 5 g; Dietary Fibre 5 g; Cholesterol 90 mg; 1270 kJ (300 Cal)

Green curry with sweet potato and eggplant

PREPARATION TIME: 15 MINUTES | TOTAL COOKING TIME: 25 MINUTES | SERVES 4–6

1 tablespoon oil

1 onion, chopped

1–2 tablespoons Thai green curry paste

1 eggplant (aubergine), quartered and sliced

375 ml (13 fl oz/1½ cups) coconut milk

250 ml (9 fl oz/1 cup) vegetable stock

6 makrut (kaffir lime) leaves

1 orange sweet potato, cut into cubes

2 teaspoons soft brown sugar

2 tablespoons lime juice

2 teaspoons lime zest

1 Heat the oil in a large wok or frying pan. Add the onion and curry paste and cook, stirring, over medium heat for 3 minutes. Add the eggplant and cook for a further 4–5 minutes, or until softened. Pour in the coconut milk and vegetable stock, bring to the boil, then reduce the heat and simmer for 5 minutes. Add the makrut leaves and sweet potato and cook, stirring occasionally, for 10 minutes, or until the eggplant and sweet potato are very tender.

2 Mix in the sugar, lime juice and lime zest until well combined with the vegetables. Season to taste with salt.

NUTRITION PER SERVE (6)
Protein 2.5 g; Fat 17 g; Carbohydrate 10 g; Dietary Fibre 3 g; Cholesterol 0.5 mg; 835 kJ (200 Cal)

Using a sharp knife, quarter and slice the eggplant before cooking until softened.

Stir-fry the onion and curry paste over medium heat for 3 minutes.

Cook, stirring occasionally, until the vegetables are tender.

Japanese pork schnitzel curry

PREPARATION TIME: 25 MINUTES | TOTAL COOKING TIME: 40 MINUTES | SERVES 4

1 tablespoon oil

1 onion, cut into thin wedges

2 large carrots, diced

1 large potato, diced

60 g (2¼ oz) Japanese curry paste block, broken into small pieces (see NOTE)

plain (all-purpose) flour, for coating

4 x 120 g (4¼ oz) pork schnitzels, pounded until thin

2 eggs, lightly beaten

150 g (5½ oz/2½ cups) Japanese breadcrumbs (panko)

oil, for deep-frying

pickled ginger, pickled daikon, umeboshi (pickled baby plums) and crisp-fried onion, to garnish

1 Heat the oil in a saucepan, add the onion, carrot and potato and cook over medium heat for 10 minutes, or until starting to brown. Add 500 ml (17 fl oz/2 cups) water and the curry paste and stir until the curry paste dissolves and the sauce has a smooth consistency. Reduce the heat and simmer for 10 minutes, or until the vegetables are cooked through.

2 Season the flour well with salt and pepper. Dip each schnitzel into the flour, shake off any excess and dip into the beaten egg, allowing any excess to drip off. Coat with the Japanese breadcrumbs by pressing each side of the schnitzel firmly into the crumbs on a plate.

3 Fill a deep heavy-based saucepan one-third full of oil and heat to 180°C (350°F), or until a cube of bread browns in 15 seconds. Cook the schnitzels, one at a time, turning once or twice, for 5 minutes, or until golden brown all over and cooked through. Drain on crumpled paper towels.

4 Slice each schnitzel and then arrange in the original shape over rice. Ladle the curry sauce over the schnitzels. Garnish with fried onions and serve with the pickles on the side.

NOTE: *Japanese curry comes in a solid block or in powder form and is available in Asian supermarkets. It varies from mild to very hot.*

NUTRITION PER SERVE
Protein 38 g; Fat 22 g; Carbohydrate 40 g; Dietary Fibre 5 g; Cholesterol 150 mg; 2145 kJ (513 Cal)

Cook the onion, carrot and potato until they are starting to brown.

Coat the schnitzels in flour, egg and then the Japanese breadcrumbs.

Prawn and coconut curry

PREPARATION TIME: 30 MINUTES I TOTAL COOKING TIME: 20 MINUTES I SERVES 4

1 onion, chopped
2 garlic cloves, crushed
1 lemongrass stem, white part only,
    finely chopped
½ teaspoon sambal oelek (South-East Asian
    chilli paste)
2 teaspoons garam masala
4 makrut (kaffir lime) leaves, finely shredded
3 tablespoons chopped coriander (cilantro)
    stems
1 tablespoon peanut oil
250 ml (9 fl oz/1 cup) chicken stock
400 ml (14 fl oz) coconut milk
1 kg (2 lb 4 oz) raw prawns (shrimp), peeled
    and deveined
1 tablespoon fish sauce

1 For the curry paste, mix the onion, garlic, lemongrass, sambal oelek, garam masala, makrut leaves, coriander stems and 2 tablespoons water in a food processor until smooth.

2 Heat the oil in a saucepan, add the curry paste and cook for 2–3 minutes, or until fragrant. Stir in the stock and coconut milk, bring to the boil, then reduce the heat and simmer for 10 minutes, or until slightly thickened.

3 Add the prawns and cook for 3–5 minutes, or until cooked through. Stir in the fish sauce.

VARIATION: *Instead of prawns, you can use bite-sized pieces of boneless ling or gemfish fillets. Cook for 3–5 minutes, or until cooked through.*

Cut the makrut leaves into fine shreds with a sharp knife.

Process the curry paste ingredients in a processor or blender until smooth.

NUTRITION PER SERVE
Protein 39 g; Fat 25.5 g; Carbohydrate 6 g; Dietary
Fibre 1.5 g; Cholesterol 261 mg; 1650 kJ (395 Cal)

Gingered duck curry

PREPARATION TIME: 30 MINUTES + 30 MINUTES REFRIGERATION + SOAKING | TOTAL COOKING TIME: 1 HOUR 30 MINUTES | SERVES 4

.8 kg (4 lb) duck

. garlic clove, crushed

. teaspoon grated fresh ginger

. tablespoon dark soy sauce

½ teaspoon sesame oil

8 dried Chinese mushrooms

5 cm (2 inch) piece fresh ginger, extra, thinly
     sliced

2 tablespoons Thai yellow curry paste

2 tablespoons chopped lemongrass, white
     part only

400 ml (14 fl oz) tin coconut milk

4 makrut (kaffir lime) leaves, shredded

100 g (3½ oz) Thai pea eggplants (aubergines)

2 teaspoons soft brown sugar

2 teaspoons fish sauce

1 tablespoon lime juice

1   Cut the duck in half by cutting down both
sides of the backbone, and through the
breastbone. Discard the backbone. Cut each
duck half into four portions, removing any fat.
Rub the duck with the combined garlic, ginger,
soy sauce and oil. Refrigerate for 30 minutes.

2   Soak the mushrooms in boiling water for
20 minutes. Drain. Remove and discard the
stalks and cut the caps in half.

3   Heat a lightly oiled pan. Brown the duck
over medium heat. Leaving only 1 tablespoon of
fat in the pan, stir-fry the extra ginger, curry
paste and lemongrass for 3 minutes. Stir in the
coconut milk, makrut leaves and 125 ml
(4 fl oz/½ cup) water. Add the duck, cover and
simmer for 45 minutes. Skim well.

4   Remove the eggplant stems; add the
eggplants to the pan with the sugar, fish sauce
and mushrooms. Simmer, partly covered, for
30 minutes, or until tender. Stir in juice to taste.

NUTRITION PER SERVE
Protein 50 g; Fat 40 g; Carbohydrate 6 g; Dietary
Fibre 1 g; Cholesterol 300 mg; 2330 kJ (560 Cal)

Cut the duck down the middle. Cut the legs and breasts in half to give eight portions.

Remove the stems from the pea eggplants and add the eggplants to the pan.

Thai chicken and potato curry

PREPARATION TIME: 20 MINUTES | TOTAL COOKING TIME: 30 MINUTES | SERVES 4–6

2 tablespoons oil

1 onion, chopped

1–2 tablespoons Thai yellow curry paste (see NOTES)

¼ teaspoon ground turmeric

420 ml (14½ fl oz/1⅔ cups) coconut milk

300 g (10½ oz) potatoes, peeled and cubed

250 g (9 oz) orange sweet potatoes, peeled and cubed

250 g (9 oz) boneless, skinless chicken thighs, diced

2 makrut (kaffir lime) leaves (see NOTES)

2 teaspoons fish sauce

2 teaspoons soft brown sugar

1 tablespoon lime juice

1 teaspoon lime zest

1 large handful coriander (cilantro) leaves

60 g (2¼ oz/⅓ cup) roasted peanuts, roughly chopped, to garnish

1 Heat the oil in a large heavy-based saucepan or wok and cook the onion until softened. Add the curry paste and turmeric and stir for 1 minute, or until aromatic.

2 Stir in the coconut milk and 250 ml (9 fl oz/1 cup) water and bring to the boil. Reduce the heat and add the potato, sweet potato, chicken and makrut leaves. Simmer for 15–20 minutes, or until the vegetables are tender and the chicken is cooked through.

3 Stir in the fish sauce, sugar, lime juice and zest and coriander leaves. Garnish with the peanuts to serve.

NOTES: *Thai yellow curry paste is not as common as the red or green but is available from most Asian food stores. Makrut leaves are now available in most supermarkets.*

NUTRITION PER SERVE (6)
Protein 10 g; Fat 35 g; Carbohydrate 15 g; Dietary Fibre 3 g; Cholesterol 40 mg; 1805 kJ (430 Cal)

Peel the orange sweet potato and chop into bite-sized pieces.

When the onion has softened, stir in the curry paste and turmeric.

Reduce the heat and add the potato, sweet potato, chicken and makrut leaves.

Rogan josh

PREPARATION TIME: 25 MINUTES | TOTAL COOKING TIME: 1 HOUR 40 MINUTES | SERVES 4–6

1 kg (2 lb 4 oz) leg of lamb, boned
1 tablespoon ghee or oil
2 onions, chopped
125 g (4½ oz/½ cup) plain yoghurt
1 teaspoon chilli powder
1 tablespoon ground coriander
2 teaspoons ground cumin
1 teaspoon ground cardamom
½ teaspoon ground cloves
1 teaspoon ground turmeric
3 garlic cloves, crushed
1 tablespoon grated fresh ginger
400 g (14 oz) tin chopped tomatoes
30 g (1 oz/¼ cup) slivered almonds
1 teaspoon garam masala
chopped coriander (cilantro) leaves,
    to garnish

1   Trim the lamb of any excess fat or sinew and cut into small cubes. Heat the ghee or oil in a large saucepan, add the onion and cook, stirring, for 5 minutes, or until soft. Stir in the yoghurt, chilli powder, ground coriander, cumin, cardamom, cloves, turmeric, garlic and ginger. Add the tomato and 1 teaspoon salt and simmer for 5 minutes.

2   Add the lamb and stir until coated. Cover and cook over low heat, stirring occasionally, for 1–1½ hours, or until the lamb is tender. Uncover and simmer until the liquid thickens.

3   Meanwhile, toast the almonds in a dry frying pan over medium heat for 3–4 minutes, shaking the pan gently, until the nuts are golden brown. Remove from the pan at once to prevent them from burning.

4   Add the garam masala to the curry and mix through well. Sprinkle the slivered almonds and coriander leaves over the top and serve.

Remove the lid from the pan and simmer until the liquid thickens.

Toast the almonds in a dry frying pan, shaking the pan gently until the nuts are golden brown.

NUTRITION PER SERVE (6)
Protein 40 g; Fat 13 g; Carbohydrate 5.5 g; Dietary Fibre 2 g; Cholesterol 122 mg; 1236 kJ (295 Cal)

Chicken dumplings in green curry

PREPARATION TIME: 25 MINUTES + 2–3 HOURS REFRIGERATION | TOTAL COOKING TIME: 35 MINUTES | SERVES 4

500 g (1 lb 2 oz) minced (ground) chicken
spring onions (scallions), finely chopped
2 tablespoons small coriander (cilantro) leaves
1 lemongrass stem, white part only,
    finely sliced
3 tablespoons fish sauce
1 teaspoon chicken stock (bouillon) powder
280 g (10 oz/1½ cups) cooked jasmine rice
1 egg, plus 1 egg white
2 teaspoons oil
2 tablespoons Thai green curry paste
2 x 400 ml (14 fl oz) tins coconut milk
4 fresh makrut (kaffir lime) leaves
2 very large handfuls basil leaves
1 tablespoon lemon juice

1   Mix together the chicken, spring onion, coriander leaves, lemongrass, 2 tablespoons of the fish sauce, stock powder and some pepper. Add the rice and mix well with your hands.

2   In a separate bowl, beat the egg and egg white with electric beaters until thick and creamy and then fold into the chicken mixture. With lightly floured hands, roll tablespoons of the mixture into balls. Place on a tray, cover and refrigerate for 2–3 hours, or until firm.

3   Heat the oil in a large frying pan, add the curry paste and stir over medium heat for 1 minute. Gradually stir in the coconut milk, then reduce the heat to a simmer. Add the makrut leaves and chicken dumplings to the sauce, cover and simmer for 25–30 minutes, stirring occasionally. Stir in the basil leaves, remaining fish sauce and lemon juice.

NUTRITION PER SERVE
Protein 40 g; Fat 50 g; Carbohydrate 65 g; Dietary Fibre 6 g; Cholesterol 130 mg; 3540 kJ (845 Cal)

Beat the egg and egg white with electric beaters until thick and creamy.

Flour your hands and roll tablespoons of the mixture into balls.

Side dishes

Rotis

PREPARATION TIME: 45 MINUTES + 2 HOURS RESTING | TOTAL COOKING TIME: 25 MINUTES | MAKES 12

375 g (13 oz/3 cups) roti flour or plain
  (all-purpose) flour
2 tablespoons softened ghee or oil, plus extra
  for frying
1 egg, lightly beaten
oil, to brush
1 egg, extra, beaten

1 Sift the flour into a large mixing bowl and stir in 1 teaspoon salt. Rub in the ghee or oil with your fingertips. Add the egg and 250 ml (9 fl oz/1 cup) warm water and mix together with a flat-bladed knife to form a moist dough. Turn the dough out onto a well-floured surface and knead for 10 minutes, or until you have a soft dough. Sprinkle the dough with more flour as necessary. Gently form the dough into a ball and brush with oil. Place in an oiled bowl, cover with plastic wrap and leave for 2 hours.

2 Remove the dough from the bowl. Working on a lightly floured surface, divide the dough into 12 pieces and roll it into even-sized balls. Take one ball and, working with oil on your fingertips, hold the ball in the air and work around the edge, pulling out the dough to form a round 15 cm (6 inches) in diameter and 3 mm (⅛ inch) thick. Lay the roti on a lightly floured surface and cover with plastic wrap so that it doesn't dry out. Repeat the process with the remaining balls.

3 Heat a frying pan over high heat and brush it with ghee or oil. Drape one of the rotis over a rolling pin and carefully place in the frying pan. Quickly brush the roti with some of the extra beaten egg. Cook for 1 minute, or until the underside is golden—this won't take long. Using a spatula, slide the roti onto a plate and brush the pan with some more ghee or oil. Return the roti to the frying pan to cook the other side. Cook the roti for 50–60 seconds, or until that side is golden. Remove from the pan and cover to keep warm while cooking the rest.

NUTRITION PER ROTI
Protein 4 g; Fat 7 g; Carbohydrate 23 g; Dietary
Fibre 1 g; Cholesterol 23 mg; 705 kJ (168 Cal)

Knead the mixture on a well-floured surface until you have a soft dough.

Pull out the dough around the edges to form a 15 cm (6 inch) round.

Drape a roti over a rolling pin and carefully place in the frying pan.

Crisp-fried onions

PREPARATION TIME: 15 MINUTES + 10 MINUTES STANDING | TOTAL COOKING TIME: 10 MINUTES | MAKES 1 CUP (SERVES 12)

1 onion, sliced paper-thin
oil, for deep-frying

1 Sit the onion on paper towels for 10 minutes.

2 Fill a deep, heavy-based saucepan one-third full of oil and heat to 160°C (315°F), or until a cube of bread dropped into the oil browns in 30–35 seconds. Cook the onion in batches for up to 1 minute, or until brown and crisp. Drain on paper towels.

3 Cool and store in an airtight container for up to 2 weeks.

NOTE: *Use as a garnish and flavour enhancer in Indonesian rice and noodle dishes.*

NUTRITION PER SERVE
Protein 0.2 g; Fat 3 g; Carbohydrate 0.5 g; Dietary Fibre 0 g; Cholesterol 0 mg; 128 kJ (30 Cal)

Slice the onion into paper-thin slices so that it will fry to a crisp finish.

Heat the oil until a cube of bread dropped in it browns in 30–35 seconds.

Cook the onions until brown and crisp and drain on crumpled paper towels.

Chapattis

PREPARATION TIME: 40 MINUTES + 50 MINUTES STANDING | TOTAL COOKING TIME: 1 HOUR 25 MINUTES | MAKES 14

280 g (10 oz/2¼ cups) atta flour (see NOTE)
melted ghee or oil, for brushing

1 Place the flour in a large bowl with a pinch of salt. Slowly add 250 ml (9 fl oz/1 cup) water, or enough to form a firm dough. Place on a lightly floured surface and knead until smooth. Cover with plastic wrap and leave for 50 minutes.

2 Divide into 14 portions and roll into 14 cm (5½ inch) circles. Heat a frying pan over medium heat and brush with the ghee or oil. Cook the chapattis one at a time over medium heat, flattening the surface, for 2–3 minutes on each side or until golden brown and bubbles appear. Serve with curries.

NOTE: *Atta flour is also known as chapatti flour and is a finely milled, low-gluten, soft-textured, wholemeal wheat flour used to make Indian flat breads. If unavailable, use plain wholemeal flour—sift it first and discard the husks. This may result in heavier, coarser bread.*

NUTRITION PER CHAPATTI
Protein 2.5 g; Fat 3 g; Carbohydrate 10 g; Dietary
Fibre 2 g; Cholesterol 0 mg; 335 kJ (80 Cal)

Add enough water to the flour mixture to form a firm dough.

Knead the dough on a lightly floured surface until it is smooth.

Flatten the surface of the chapatti with a spatula while cooking.

Mango chutney

PREPARATION TIME: 20 MINUTES | TOTAL COOKING TIME: 1 HOUR 5 MINUTES | MAKES 3 CUPS (SERVES 36)

3 large green mangoes
½ teaspoon garam masala
330 g (11¾ oz/1½ cups) sugar
250 ml (9 fl oz/1 cup) white vinegar
2 small red chillies, seeded and
    finely chopped
1 tablespoon finely grated fresh ginger
80 g (2¾ oz/½ cup) finely chopped pitted
    dates

1 Cut the cheeks from the rounded side of each mango and use a large spoon to scoop out the flesh. Cut the remaining flesh from around the sides of the seed and chop all the flesh into large slices. Sprinkle with salt.

2 Mix together the garam masala and sugar. Place in a large saucepan with the vinegar. Bring to the boil, then reduce the heat and simmer for 5 minutes.

3 Add the mango slices, chilli, ginger and dates and simmer for 1 hour, or until the mango is tender. Stir often during cooking to prevent the chutney from sticking and burning on the bottom, especially towards the end of the cooking time.

4 Spoon immediately into sterilised jars (see NOTE) and seal. Turn the jars upside down for 2 minutes, then invert and leave to cool. Label and date. Will keep for up to six months.

NOTE: *To sterilise jars, preheat the oven to very low 120°C (235°F/Gas ½). Thoroughly wash the jars and lids in hot soapy water (or preferably in a dishwasher) and rinse well with hot water. Put the jars on baking trays and place them in the oven for 20 minutes, or until they are fully dried and you are ready to use them. Do not dry the jars, or the lids, with a tea towel (dish towel).*

HINT: *Mango chutney is great with almost any Indian curry, especially the hotter ones. It also tastes delicious with roast lamb or beef.*

NUTRITION PER SERVE
Protein 0.2 g; Fat 0 g; Carbohydrate 13 g; Dietary
Fibre 0.5 g; Cholesterol mg; 212 kJ (50 Cal)

Use a large metal spoon to scoop out the mango flesh from the cheeks.

Simmer the mixture for 1 hour, or until the mango is tender.

Naan

PREPARATION TIME: 15 MINUTES + 2 HOURS RESTING | TOTAL COOKING TIME: 10 MINUTES | MAKES 8

500 g (1 lb 2 oz/4 cups) plain
   (all-purpose) flour
1 teaspoon baking powder
½ teaspoon bicarbonate of soda (baking soda)
1 egg, beaten
125 g (4½ oz/½ cup) plain yoghurt
4 tablespoons ghee or butter, melted
250 ml (9 fl oz/1 cup) milk

1 Preheat the oven to 200°C (400°F/Gas 6). Lightly grease two 28 x 33 cm (11¼ x 13 inch) baking trays. Sift together the flour, baking powder, bicarbonate of soda and 1 teaspoon salt. Mix in the egg, yoghurt and 1 tablespoon of the ghee or butter and gradually add enough of the milk to form a soft dough. Cover with a damp cloth and leave in a warm place for 2 hours.

2 Knead the dough on a well-floured surface for 2–3 minutes, or until smooth. Divide into eight portions and roll each one into an oval 15 cm (6 inches) long. Brush with water and place, wet side down, on the baking trays. Brush with the rest of the melted ghee or butter and bake for 8–10 minutes, or until golden brown. Serve with Indian curries.

VARIATION: *To make garlic naan, crush 6 garlic cloves and sprinkle evenly over the dough prior to baking.*

Mix all the ingredients together with enough milk to form a soft dough.

Knead the dough on a well-floured surface until it is smooth.

NUTRITION PER NAAN
Protein 10 g; Fat 12 g; Carbohydrate 48 g; Dietary Fibre 2.5 g; Cholesterol 55 mg; 1418 kJ (340 Cal)

Puri

PREPARATION TIME: 50 MINUTES + 50 MINUTES STANDING | TOTAL COOKING TIME: 20 MINUTES | MAKES 18

225 g (8 oz/1½ cups) wholemeal flour
125 g (4½ oz/1 cup) plain (all-purpose) flour
1 tablespoon ghee or oil
oil, for deep-frying

1 Sift the flours together with a pinch of salt. Discard the husks. Rub in the ghee or oil with your fingertips. Gradually add 170 ml (5½ fl oz/⅔ cup) water to form a firm dough. Knead on a lightly floured surface until smooth. Cover with plastic wrap and leave for 50 minutes.

2 Divide into 18 portions and roll into circles 3 mm (⅛ inch) thick and 14 cm (5½ inches) in diameter.

3 Fill a deep heavy-based saucepan one-third full of oil and heat to 180°C (350°F), or until a cube of bread dropped into the oil browns in 15 seconds. Add the puri one at a time and cook, spooning oil over the top, for 30–60 seconds, or until puffed. Turn and cook until golden brown. Drain on paper towels. Serve immediately with Indian curries.

NUTRITION PER PURI
Protein 2 g; Fat 4 g; Carbohydrate 12 g; Dietary Fibre 1.5 g; Cholesterol 3 mg; 360 kJ (85 Cal)

Knead the dough on a lightly foured surface until smooth.

Divide the dough into 18 portions and roll each into a 14 cm (5½ inch) circle.

Cook the puri, spooning oil over them until they puff up and turn golden brown.

Cucumber raita

PREPARATION TIME: 5 MINUTES | TOTAL COOKING TIME: 1 MINUTE | MAKES 1⅓ CUPS (SERVES 10)

2 Lebanese (short) cucumbers, peeled, seeded, finely chopped
250 g (9 oz/1 cup) plain yoghurt
1 teaspoon ground cumin
1 teaspoon mustard seeds
½ teaspoon grated fresh ginger
paprika, to garnish

1 Mix together the cucumber and yoghurt in a large bowl.

2 Dry-fry the ground cumin and mustard seeds in a small frying pan over medium heat for 1 minute, or until fragrant and lightly browned, then add to the yoghurt mixture. Stir in the ginger, season to taste with salt and pepper and mix together well. Garnish with the paprika. Serve chilled. Will keep in an airtight container in the refrigerator for up to three days.

VARIATIONS: *Add 2 tablespoons chopped fresh coriander (cilantro) leaves or mint leaves to the cucumber raita. Or, replace the cucumber with 500 g (1 lb 2 oz) English spinach. Bring a large saucepan of water to the boil, add the spinach and cook for 1–2 minutes. Drain the spinach, squeezing out any excess water. Chop finely and combine with the yoghurt.*

To make a tomato raita, replace the cucumber with 2 medium, seeded, diced tomatoes. Add 1 tablespoon very finely chopped onion as well.

NUTRITION PER SERVE
Protein 1 g; Fat 0.5 g; Carbohydrate 1 g; Dietary Fibre 0 g; Cholesterol 4.5 mg; 54 kJ (13 Cal)

Place the cucumber and yoghurt in a bowl and mix together.

Dry-fry the ground cumin and mustard seeds until fragrant and lightly browned.

Sambal oelek (hot chilli paste)

PREPARATION TIME: 10 MINUTES | TOTAL COOKING TIME: 15 MINUTES | MAKES 1 CUP (SERVES 48)

200 g (7 oz) small fresh red chillies
1 teaspoon sugar
1 tablespoon vinegar
1 tablespoon oil

1 Roughly chop the chillies, wearing gloves to protect your hands, then place in a saucepan with 125 ml (4 fl oz/½ cup) water and bring to the boil. Reduce the heat and simmer, covered, for 15 minutes.

2 Pour the chilli and the cooking liquid into a food processor or blender and add the sugar, vinegar, oil and 1 teaspoon salt. Finely chop. Pour immediately into a sterilised jar and carefully seal. Leave to cool. Will keep in the fridge for a month.

NOTE: *Sambal oelek is a very hot paste, so use it sparingly. It is used as a relish in Indonesian and Malaysian cooking and can also be used as a substitute for fresh chillies in most recipes.*

NUTRITION PER SERVE (1 TEASPOON)
Protein 0 g; Fat 0 g; Carbohydrate 0 g; Dietary Fibre 0 g; Cholesterol 0 mg; 23 kJ (5.5 Cal)

Wear gloves while chopping the chillies to protect your hands.

Process all the ingredients in a food processor until finely chopped.

Pour the mixture immediately into a sterilised jar. It can then be kept for up to a month.

Coriander chutney

PREPARATION TIME: 10 MINUTES | TOTAL COOKING TIME: NIL | MAKES 1¼ CUPS (SERVES 9)

90 g (3¼ oz/1 bunch) fresh coriander
    (cilantro), including the roots,
    roughly chopped
3 tablespoons desiccated (grated dried)
    coconut
1 tablespoon soft brown sugar
1 tablespoon grated fresh ginger
1 small onion, chopped
2 tablespoons lemon juice
1–2 small green chillies, seeded

1   Place all the ingredients and 1 teaspoon salt
in a food processor and process for 1 minute,
or until finely chopped. Refrigerate until ready to
serve. Serve chilled.

NOTE: *Chutneys are spicy, vegetarian Indian
relishes eaten as side dishes. They are often used
to perk up plain dishes such as dhal or rice and are
traditionally made fresh for each meal.*

VARIATIONS: *There are numerous variations,
depending on region and tastes. Try substituting
1 bunch of roughly chopped fresh mint leaves
for the coriander in this recipe, or add 5 roughly
chopped spring onions (scallions) (including the
green part) instead of the onion.*

*If you prefer more fire in your chutney, do not
remove the seeds from the chillies. It is the seeds
and white fibrous tissue inside the chillies that
contain most of the heat.*

Roughly chop the fresh coriander leaves, stems
and roots.

Place all the ingredients in a food processor and
mix until finely chopped.

NUTRITION PER SERVE
Protein 0.2 g; Fat 1 g; Carbohydrate 2 g; Dietary
Fibre 0.5 g; Cholesterol 0.5 mg; 75 kJ (18 Cal)

Dhal

PREPARATION TIME: 15 MINUTES | TOTAL COOKING TIME: 35 MINUTES | SERVES 4–6

200 g (7 oz) red lentils

5 cm (2 inch) piece fresh ginger, cut into
    3 slices

½ teaspoon ground turmeric

1 tablespoon ghee or oil

2 garlic cloves, crushed

1 onion, finely chopped

½ teaspoon yellow mustard seeds

pinch of asafoetida (optional)

1 teaspoon cumin seeds

1 teaspoon ground coriander

2 green chillies, halved lengthways

2 tablespoons lemon juice

1 tablespoon chopped coriander (cilantro)
    leaves

1 Put the lentils and 750 ml (26 fl oz/3 cups) water in a saucepan and bring to the boil. Reduce the heat, add the ginger and turmeric and simmer, covered, for 20 minutes, or until tender. Stir occasionally to prevent sticking. Remove the ginger and stir in ½ teaspoon salt.

2 Heat the ghee or oil in a frying pan, add the garlic, onion and mustard seeds, and cook over medium heat for 5 minutes, or until the onion is golden. Add the asafoetida, cumin seeds, ground coriander and chilli and cook for 2 minutes.

3 Add the onion mixture to the lentils and stir gently. Add 125 ml (4 fl oz/½ cup) water, reduce the heat to low and cook for 5 minutes. Stir in the lemon juice and season. Sprinkle with the coriander. Serve as a side dish with Indian curries.

NUTRITION PER SERVE (6)
Protein 9 g; Fat 4 g; Carbohydrate 13 g; Dietary Fibre 5 g; Cholesterol 8 mg; 505 kJ (120 Cal)

Add the ginger and turmeric to the lentils and cook until the lentils are tender.

Cook the garlic, onion and mustard seeds until the onion is golden.

Desserts

Banana tempura with green tea ice cream

PREPARATION TIME: 30 MINUTES + FREEZING | TOTAL COOKING TIME: 25 MINUTES | SERVES 4

ICE CREAM
10 g (¼ oz/⅓ cup) Japanese green tea leaves
500 ml (17 fl oz/2 cups) milk
6 egg yolks
125 g (4¼ oz/½ cup) caster (superfine) sugar
500 ml (17 fl oz/2 cups) pouring
   (whipping) cream

BANANA TEMPURA
oil, for deep-frying
1 egg
185 ml (6 fl oz/¾ cup) iced water
90 g (3¼ oz/⅔ cup) tempura flour
4 small bananas
caster (superfine) sugar and honey, to serve

NUTRITION PER SERVE
Protein 16 g; Fat 77 g; Carbohydrate 80 g; Dietary
Fibre 3.5 g; Cholesterol 494 mg; 4413 kJ (1054 Cal)

1   Combine the tea leaves and milk in a saucepan and bring to simmering point very slowly over low heat. Set aside for 5 minutes before straining.

2   Whisk the egg yolks and sugar in a heatproof bowl until thick and pale, then add the infused milk. Place the bowl over a saucepan of simmering water, making sure that the base of the bowl is not touching the water. Stir the custard until thick enough to coat the back of a spoon, then remove from the heat and cool slightly. Add the cream.

3   Pour the mixture into a metal tray and freeze for 1½–2 hours, or until just frozen around the edges. Transfer to a chilled bowl, beat with electric beaters until thick and creamy, then return to the metal tray. Repeat the freezing and beating twice more. Transfer to a storage container, cover the surface with baking paper and freeze overnight.

4   Heat the oil in a deep-fryer or heavy-based saucepan to 170°C (325°F), or until a cube of bread browns in 20 seconds. Mix together the egg and water in a bowl, then stir in the tempura flour. Do not whisk the batter—it must be lumpy.

5   Split the bananas lengthways, then crossways. Dip the banana quarters into the batter and deep-fry a few at a time for about 2 minutes, or until crisp and golden. Drain on paper towels and sprinkle with caster sugar. Serve with a scoop of ice cream and drizzle with warmed honey.

Whisk the egg yolks and sugar in a heatproof bowl until thick and pale.

Stir the custard until it is thick enough to coat the back of a spoon.

Deep-fry the bananas until crisp and golden, then drain on paper towels.

Mango ice cream

PREPARATION TIME: 20 MINUTES + FREEZING I TOTAL COOKING TIME: NIL I SERVES 4

3 fresh mangoes
125 g (4½ oz) caster (superfine) sugar
3 tablespoons mango nectar
300 ml (10½ fl oz) pouring (whipping) cream

1   Peel the mangoes, cut into pieces and purée in a food processor until smooth. Transfer to a bowl and add the sugar and nectar. Stir until the sugar has dissolved.

2   Beat the cream until stiff peaks form and then gently fold into the mango.

3   Spoon the mixture into a shallow tray, cover and freeze for 1½ hours or until half-frozen. Spoon into a food processor and mix for 30 seconds, or until smooth. Return to the tray or a plastic container, cover and freeze completely. Remove the ice cream from the freezer 15 minutes before serving, to allow it to soften a little. Serve with fresh mango.

STORAGE: *Freeze the ice cream for at least eight hours—it can be kept in the freezer for up to three weeks.*

VARIATION: *Stir in some toasted, desiccated (grated dried) coconut before freezing the ice cream completely.*

NUTRITION PER SERVE
Protein 2 g; Fat 35 g; Carbohydrate 80 g; Dietary Fibre 5 g; Cholesterol 100 mg; 2150 kJ (640 Cal)

Put the mangoes in a food processor and mix until smooth.

Fold the whipped cream through the mango with a metal spoon to keep the volume.

Pour the processed ice cream back into the tray and freeze completely.

Fruit salad

PREPARATION TIME: 25 MINUTES + CHILLING | TOTAL COOKING TIME: 20 MINUTES | SERVES 6

1 small pineapple, peeled and chopped
1 papaya, peeled and chopped
3 starfruit, sliced
8 rambutans, peeled and seeded
500 g (1 lb 2 oz/2¼ cups) caster
    (superfine) sugar
2 tablespoons lemon or lime juice
5 cm (2 inch) strip lemon or lime zest
mint leaves, to garnish

1 Place the prepared fruit in a large bowl, cover and chill for at least 30 minutes.

2 Place the caster sugar and 500 ml (17 fl oz/ 2 cups) water in a saucepan. Stir over low heat, without boiling, for 5 minutes, or until the sugar has dissolved. Add the juice and zest to the pan and bring the mixture to the boil. Boil without stirring for 10 minutes, or until the syrup has thickened slightly. Remove the zest from the pan and set the mixture aside to cool.

3 Just prior to serving, pour over enough cooled syrup to coat the fruit and carefully fold it through. Arrange the fruit in a bowl or hollowed-out melon. Garnish with mint leaves.

STORAGE: *The syrup can be prepared a day ahead, covered and refrigerated.*

NUTRITION PER SERVE
Protein 1 g; Fat 0 g; Carbohydrate 96 g; Dietary
Fibre 4 g; Cholesterol 0 mg; 1575 kJ (375 Cal)

Peel the rambutans and use your fingers to remove the seeds.

Add the juice and zest and boil the syrup for 10 minutes, or until it thickens slightly.

Just before serving, pour over enough of the cooled syrup to coat the fruit.

Coconut ice cream

PREPARATION TIME: 10 MINUTES + FREEZING | TOTAL COOKING TIME: 15 MINUTES | SERVES 4

425 ml (15 fl oz) tin coconut cream

375 ml (13 fl oz/1½ cups) pouring
(whipping) cream

2 eggs

2 egg yolks

125 g (4½ oz) caster (superfine) sugar

1 teaspoon vanilla essence

mint leaves and toasted, shredded coconut,
to garnish

1 Put the coconut cream and cream in a saucepan. Stir over medium heat, without boiling, for 2–3 minutes. Cover and keep warm. Place the eggs, egg yolks, sugar, ¼ teaspoon salt and vanilla in a large heatproof bowl. Beat with electric beaters for 2–3 minutes, or until frothy and thickened. Place the bowl over a saucepan of simmering water.

2 Continue to beat the egg mixture while gradually adding the warm coconut cream mixture, a little at a time, until all the coconut mixture is added. This will take about 10 minutes—continue until the custard thickens. The mixture will be the consistency of thin cream and should easily coat the back of a spoon. Do not boil or it will curdle.

3 Cover and set aside to cool. Stir the mixture occasionally while it is cooling. When cool, pour into a shallow tray, cover and freeze for about 1½ hours, or until half-frozen.

4 Quickly spoon the mixture into a food processor and process for 30 seconds, or until smooth. Return to the tray or place in plastic containers; cover and freeze completely. Serve garnished with mint and coconut.

STORAGE: *Will keep for up to three weeks in the freezer. Allow to stand at room temperature for 10–15 minutes before serving.*

NUTRITION PER SERVE
Protein 5 g; Fat 60 g; Carbohydrate 40 g; Dietary Fibre 2 g; Cholesterol 140 mg; 3000 kJ (900 Cal)

Beat the mixture until it is thick and frothy, using electric beaters.

Cook the coconut mixture until it easily coats the back of a spoon.

Pour the cooled mixture into a shallow tray, cover and freeze until half frozen.

Sago pudding

PREPARATION TIME: 20 MINUTES + 1 HOUR SOAKING + 2 HOURS REFRIGERATION I TOTAL COOKING TIME: 20 MINUTES I SERVES 6

195 g (7 oz/1 cup) sago
185 g (6½ oz/1 cup) soft brown sugar
250 ml (9 fl oz/1 cup) coconut cream,
 well chilled

1 Soak the sago in 750 ml (26 fl oz/3 cups) water for 1 hour. Pour into a saucepan, add 2 tablespoons of the brown sugar and bring to the boil over low heat, stirring constantly. Reduce the heat and simmer, stirring occasionally, for 10 minutes. Cover and cook over low heat, stirring occasionally, for 2–3 minutes, until the mixture is thick and the sago grains are translucent.

2 Half-fill six rinsed (still wet) 125 ml (4 fl oz/½ cup) moulds with the sago mixture and refrigerate for 2 hours, or until set.

3 Combine the remaining brown sugar with 250 ml (9 fl oz/1 cup) water in a small saucepan and cook over low heat, stirring constantly, until the sugar dissolves. Simmer for 5–7 minutes, until the syrup thickens. Remove from the heat and cool. To serve, unmould and top with a little of the sugar syrup and coconut cream.

STORAGE: *The syrup can be made up to a day in advance, and stored covered and refrigerated.*

NUTRITION PER SERVE
Protein 3 g; Fat 9 g; Carbohydrate 60 g; Dietary Fibre 2 g; Cholesterol 0 mg; 1340 kJ (320 Cal)

Cook until the mixture thickens and the sago grains are translucent.

Sticky black rice

PREPARATION TIME: 20 MINUTES + OVERNIGHT SOAKING | TOTAL COOKING TIME: 40 MINUTES | SERVES 8

400 g (14 oz/2 cups) black rice
500 ml (17 fl oz/2 cups) coconut milk
80 g (2¾ oz) grated palm sugar (jaggery)
3 tablespoons caster (superfine) sugar
3 fresh pandan leaves, shredded and knotted
3 tablespoons coconut cream
3 tablespoons creamed corn (optional)

1   Place the rice in a large glass or ceramic bowl and cover with water. Soak for at least 8 hours or overnight. Drain and transfer to a medium saucepan with 1 litre (35 fl oz/4 cups) water. Bring slowly to the boil, stirring frequently, and simmer for 20 minutes, or until tender. Drain.

2   In a large heavy-based saucepan, heat the coconut milk until almost boiling. Add the palm sugar, caster sugar and pandan leaves and stir until the sugars have dissolved. Add the rice and stir for 3–4 minutes without boiling.

3   Turn off the heat, cover the pan and allow to stand for 15 minutes to allow the flavours to be absorbed. Remove the pandan leaves. Serve warm with coconut cream, and creamed corn, if desired.

NOTE: *Black rice, palm sugar and pandan leaves are all available from Asian food speciality stores.*

NUTRITION PER SERVE
Protein 5 g; Fat 14 g; Carbohydrate 50 g; Dietary Fibre 3 g; Cholesterol 0 mg; 1445 kJ (345 Cal)

Soak the black rice in water for at least 8 hours, or overnight.

Sansrival (Philippine cashew meringue cake)

PREPARATION TIME: 40 MINUTES + COOLING | TOTAL COOKING TIME: 45 MINUTES | SERVES 8–10

CASHEW MERINGUE
300 g (10½ oz) cashew nuts
8 egg whites
375 g (13 oz/1⅔ cups) caster
    (superfine) sugar
2 teaspoons vanilla essence
2 teaspoons white vinegar

FILLING
250 g (9 oz/1 cup) unsalted butter, softened
125 g (4½ oz/1 cup) icing
    (confectioners') sugar
4 tablespoons crème de cacao
500 ml (17 fl oz/2 cups) pouring
    (whipping) cream
1 tablespoon orange liqueur
2 teaspoons vanilla essence
chocolate or cocoa, for decoration (optional)

NUTRITION PER SERVE (10)
Protein 8 g; Fat 57 g; Carbohydrate 60 g; Dietary
Fibre 2 g; Cholesterol 130 mg; 3160 kJ (760 Cal)

1   To make the meringue, preheat the oven to 180°C (350°F/Gas 4). Spread the cashews on a baking tray and toast them in the oven for 5 minutes, or until golden, stirring occasionally to turn them over. Remove from the oven, allow to cool and then process in short bursts in a food processor, until finely ground. Reduce the oven temperature to 150°C (300°F/Gas 2). Line four oven trays with non-stick baking paper and draw a 21 cm (8¼ inch) diameter circle onto each piece.

2   Beat the egg whites in a large bowl until soft peaks form. Gradually add the caster sugar, beating well after each addition, until the whites are thick and glossy. Using a metal spoon, fold in the vanilla, vinegar and cashews. Divide the mixture evenly among the circles and spread it to the edge of each circle. Bake the meringues for about 45 minutes. Turn the oven off and allow the meringues to cool in the oven, leaving the oven door ajar.

3   To make the filling, beat the butter, icing sugar and crème de cacao until light and creamy. In a separate bowl, beat the cream, orange liqueur and vanilla essence until soft peaks form.

4   Place a meringue circle on a serving plate and spread with half of the crème de cacao mixture. Top with another meringue circle and spread with half of the orange cream mixture. Repeat with the remaining circles and mixtures. Decorate the top of the cake with chocolate curls and dust lightly with cocoa.

Fold the vanilla essence, vinegar and ground cashews into the egg whites.

Use a spatula to spread the meringue mixture to the edge of each circle.

Spread the second layer of meringue with half the orange cream.

Caramel sticky rice

PREPARATION TIME: 40 MINUTES + OVERNIGHT SOAKING | TOTAL COOKING TIME: 1 HOUR 15 MINUTES | SERVES 4

400 g (14 oz/2 cups) glutinous white rice
250 ml (9 fl oz/1 cup) coconut milk
90 g (3¼ oz) grated palm sugar (jaggery)
starfruit, finely sliced
3 tablespoons coconut cream
1 tablespoon sesame seeds, toasted

1 Rinse the rice until the water runs clear. Put into a glass bowl, cover with water and soak overnight, then drain.

2 Line a bamboo steamer with baking paper or a damp tea towel (dish towel) and place it over a water-filled wok. Spread the rice over the base of the steamer, fold the sides of the paper over the rice and cover with another sheet of paper. Tuck it in so the rice is completely encased and cover with the bamboo lid. Steam over medium heat for 50 minutes, or until just cooked, refilling the water whenever necessary.

3 Stir the coconut milk, palm sugar and ¼ teaspoon salt in a small saucepan until boiling. Reduce the heat and simmer for 15 minutes, or until a thick caramel forms.

4 Pour one-quarter of the caramel over the rice, fork it through, cover again with the paper and lid and steam for 5 minutes. Repeat with the remaining caramel, cooking the rice until plump and sticky. Press into a square dish, leave to stand and then cut into diamonds, or form into balls and serve warm with starfruit, coconut cream and sesame seeds.

Grate the palm sugar on the large holes of a metal grater.

Cover the rice with baking paper, tucking in the sides to encase the rice.

NUTRITION PER SERVE
Protein 10 g; Fat 20 g; Carbohydrate 100 g; Dietary Fibre 4 g; Cholesterol 0 mg; 2555 kJ (610 Cal)

Carrot milk pudding

PREPARATION TIME: 5 MINUTES | TOTAL COOKING TIME: 1 HOUR | SERVES 6

litre (35 fl oz/4 cups) milk
25 g (8 oz/1½ cups) grated carrot
0 g (2¼ oz/½ cup) sultanas (golden raisins)
25 g (4½ oz/½ cup) caster (superfine) sugar
¼ teaspoon ground cinnamon
¼ teaspoon ground cardamom
0 ml (2½ fl oz/⅓ cup) pouring
   (whipping) cream
tablespoons shelled, chopped pistachios

1   Pour the milk into a large, heavy-based saucepan. Place over medium heat and stir as it comes to the boil. Reduce the heat to low and leave until the milk reduces to about half its original volume. Stir occasionally to prevent it from catching on the pan bottom.

2   Add the carrot and sultanas and cook a further 15 minutes.

3   Add the sugar, cinnamon, cardamom and cream and cook, stirring, until the sugar dissolves. Serve warm, sprinkled with pistachios. This pudding doesn't keep well and should be served immediately.

HINT: *Indian sweets are often made from reduced milk. A heavy saucepan and an even distribution of heat for boiling down the milk are important.*

NUTRITION PER SERVE
Protein 8 g; Fat 15 g; Carbohydrate 18 g; Dietary Fibre 2 g; Cholesterol 40 mg; 980 kJ (235 Cal)

Stir the milk as it comes to the boil and then leave over low heat until reduced.

Add the carrot and sultanas to the milk and cook for a further 15 minutes.

Add the sugar, cinnamon, cardamom and cream and cook until the sugar dissolves.

Banana and coconut pancakes

PREPARATION TIME: 20 MINUTES | TOTAL COOKING TIME: 30 MINUTES | SERVES 6

40 g (1½ oz/⅓ cup) plain (all-purpose) flour
2 tablespoons rice flour
60 g (2¼ oz/¼ cup) caster (superfine) sugar
25 g (1 oz/¼ cup) desiccated (grated dried) coconut
250 ml (9 fl oz/1 cup) coconut milk
1 egg, lightly beaten
60 g (2¼ oz/¼ cup) butter
4 large bananas
60 g (2¼ oz/⅓ cup) soft brown sugar
80 ml (2½ fl oz/⅓ cup) lime juice
1 tablespoon shredded coconut, toasted, for serving
strips of lime zest, for serving

NUTRITION PER SERVE
Protein 4 g; Fat 14 g; Carbohydrate 30 g; Dietary Fibre 3 g; Cholesterol 30 mg; 1083 kJ (260 Cal)

1 Sift the flours into a bowl. Add the sugar and coconut and mix through with a spoon. Make a well in the centre, pour in the combined coconut milk and egg and beat until smooth.

2 Heat a non-stick frying pan and melt a little butter in it. Pour 3 tablespoons of the pancake mixture into the pan and cook over medium heat until the underside is golden.

3 Turn the pancake over and cook the other side. Transfer to a plate and cover with a tea towel (dish towel) to keep warm while cooking the rest, buttering the pan when necessary. Keep warm while preparing the bananas.

4 Cut the bananas diagonally into thick slices. Heat the remaining butter in the pan, add the bananas and toss until coated. Cook over medium heat until the bananas start to soften and brown. Sprinkle with the brown sugar and shake the pan gently until the sugar has melted. Stir in the lime juice. Divide the bananas among the pancakes and fold over to enclose. Sprinkle with toasted coconut and strips of lime zest.

Beat the pancake mixture thoroughly, until it is completely smooth.

When the pancakes are cooked, transfer them to a plate and keep them warm.

Toss the bananas gently until they are well coated with butter.

Ginger and lychee jelly

PREPARATION TIME: 10 MINUTES + 4 HOURS SETTING | TOTAL COOKING TIME: 5 MINUTES | SERVES 6

500 g (1 lb 2 oz) tin lychees
500 ml (17 fl oz/2 cups) clear apple juice
 (no added sugar)
80 ml (2½ fl oz/⅓ cup) strained lime juice
2 tablespoons caster (superfine) sugar
5 cm (2 inch) piece fresh ginger, thinly sliced
4 sheets gelatine
mint, to garnish

1   Drain the syrup from the lychees and put 250 ml (9 fl oz/1 cup) of the syrup in a saucepan. Discard the remaining syrup. Add the apple juice, lime juice, sugar and ginger to the pan. Bring to the boil, then reduce the heat and simmer for 5 minutes. Strain into a heatproof bowl.

2   Place the gelatine sheets in a large bowl of cold water and soak for 2 minutes, or until they soften. Squeeze out the excess water, then add to the syrup. Stir until completely dissolved. Leave to cool.

3   Pour 2 tablespoons of the jelly into each of six 150 ml (5 fl oz) wine glasses or small bowls and divide the lychees among the glasses. Refrigerate until set. Spoon the remaining jelly over the fruit and refrigerate until set. Before serving, garnish with mint leaves.

After soaking, squeeze the sheets of gelatine to remove any excess water.

Divide the lychees among wine glasses gently dropping them into the jelly.

NUTRITION PER SERVE
Protein 1 g; Fat 0 g; Carbohydrate 31 g; Dietary Fibre 0.5 g; Cholesterol 0 mg; 530 kJ (125 Cal)

Spicy coconut custard

PREPARATION TIME: 20 MINUTES | TOTAL COOKING TIME: 1 HOUR | SERVES 8

2 cinnamon sticks
1 teaspoon ground nutmeg
2 teaspoons whole cloves
300 ml (10½ fl oz) pouring (whipping) cream
125 g (4½ oz) chopped palm sugar (jaggery)
280 ml (10 fl oz) tin coconut milk
3 eggs, lightly beaten
2 egg yolks, lightly beaten

1   Preheat the oven to 160°C (315°F/
Gas 2–3). Put the spices, cream and 250 ml
(9 fl oz/1 cup) water in a saucepan. Bring to
simmering point, then reduce the heat to very
low and leave for 5 minutes to allow the spices to
flavour the liquid.

2   Add the sugar and coconut milk to the
pan, return to low heat and stir until the sugar
has dissolved.

3   Whisk the eggs and egg yolks together. Pour
the spiced mixture over the eggs and stir well.
Strain, discarding the whole spices. Pour the
custard mixture into eight 125 ml (4 fl oz/
½ cup) dishes. Put the dishes in a roasting tin
and pour enough boiling water into the tin to
come halfway up the sides of the dishes. Bake for
40–45 minutes.

4   Poke a knife in the centre of one of the
custards to check if they are set—the mixture
should be only slightly wobbly. Remove the
custards from the roasting tin and serve hot
or chilled.

STORAGE: *The custards will keep, covered and
refrigerated, for up to three days.*

Strain the custard into a pitcher and discard the
whole spices.

Insert a knife in the centre of one of the custards
to check if they are set.

NUTRITION PER SERVE
Protein 5 g; Fat 26 g; Carbohydrate 3 g; Dietary
Fibre 0 g; Cholesterol 166 mg; 1080 kJ (260 Cal)

Basics—curry pastes and more

Curry pastes and powders

Balti masala paste

MAKES 1 CUP

Separately dry-fry the following ingredients in a small frying pan over medium heat, for 2–3 minutes, or until just starting to become fragrant: 4 tablespoons coriander seeds, 2 tablespoons cumin seeds, 2 crumbled cinnamon sticks, 2 teaspoons fennel seeds, 2 teaspoons black mustard seeds, 2 teaspoons cardamom seeds, 1 teaspoon fenugreek seeds and 6 cloves. Transfer all the spices to a food processor or mortar and pestle and mix or grind to a powder. Add 4 fresh bay leaves, 20 fresh curry leaves, 1 tablespoon ground turmeric, 2 crushed garlic cloves, 1 tablespoon grated fresh ginger, 1½ teaspoons chilli powder and 185 ml (6 fl oz/¾ cup) vinegar and mix well. Heat 125 ml (4 fl oz/½ cup) of oil in the pan, add the paste and cook, stirring, for 5 minutes. Stir in 60 ml (2 fl oz/¼ cup) of vinegar. Pour into clean, warm jars and seal. Will keep in the refrigerator for 1 month.

Chu chee curry paste

MAKES ½ CUP

Preheat the oven to 180°C (350°F/Gas 4). Soak 10 large dried red chillies in boiling water for 10 minutes. Drain, remove the seeds and roughly chop. Place 1 teaspoon coriander seeds, 1 tablespoon shrimp paste (wrapped in foil) and 1 tablespoon white peppercorns on a foil-lined baking tray and bake for 5 minutes, or until fragrant. Unwrap the paste. Mix the above ingredients in a food processor or mortar and pestle, and add the following: 10 finely shredded makrut (kaffir lime) leaves, 10 chopped red Asian shallots (eschalots), 2 teaspoons finely grated makrut (kaffir lime) zest, 1 tablespoon chopped coriander (cilantro) stem and root, 1 finely chopped lemongrass stem (white part only), 3 tablespoons chopped galangal, 1 tablespoon chopped krachai (optional) and 6 chopped garlic cloves. Mix all the ingredients to a smooth paste. You may need to use a little lemon juice if the paste is too thick. Will keep in an airtight container in the refrigerator for up to 1 month.

Garam masala

MAKES ½ CUP

Dry-fry the following ingredients separately in a frying pan over medium heat, for 2–3 minutes, or until just becoming fragrant: 2 tablespoons of coriander seeds, 1½ tablespoons cardamom pods, 1 tablespoon cumin seeds, 2 teaspoons whole black peppercorns, 1 teaspoon whole cloves and 3 cinnamon sticks. Remove the cardamom pods, crush with the handle of a heavy knife and remove the seeds. Discard the pods. Place the fried spices, cardamom seeds and 1 grated nutmeg in a food processor, blender or mortar and pestle, and process or grind to a powder. Store in an airtight container in a cool, dark place.

General-purpose Indian curry powder

MAKES ⅓ CUP

Dry-fry the following ingredients separately in a small frying pan, over medium heat for 2–3 minutes, or until fragrant: 2 teaspoons cumin seeds, 2 teaspoons coriander seeds, 2 teaspoons fenugreek seeds, 1 teaspoon yellow mustard seeds, 1 teaspoon black peppercorns, 1 teaspoon cloves, 1 teaspoon chilli powder, 2 teaspoons ground turmeric, ½ teaspoon ground cinnamon and ½ teaspoon ground cardamom. Place the seeds in a spice grinder, mortar and pestle or small food processor with a fine blade and grind to a fine powder. Place in a small bowl with the pre-ground spices and mix together well. Store in an airtight container in a cool, dark place.

Madras curry paste

MAKES ½ CUP

Place the following ingredients in a small bowl and mix together well: 2½ tablespoons dry-roasted, ground coriander seeds, 1 tablespoon dry-roasted ground cumin seeds, 1 teaspoon brown mustard seeds, ½ teaspoon cracked black peppercorns, 1 teaspoon chilli powder, 1 teaspoon ground turmeric, 2 crushed garlic cloves, 2 teaspoons of grated fresh ginger and 1 teaspoon salt. Add 3–4 tablespoons of white vinegar and mix to a smooth paste. Will keep in a clean airtight container in the refrigerator for up to a month.

Massaman curry paste

MAKES ½ CUP

Preheat the oven to 180°C (350°F/Gas 4). Soak 10 dried large red chillies in boiling water for 10 minutes, drain, remove the seeds and roughly chop. Put the following ingredients in a dish and bake for 5 minutes, or until fragrant: 3 cardamom pods, 1 teaspoon cumin seeds, 1 tablespoon coriander seeds, ¼ teaspoon black peppercorns, 1 teaspoon shrimp paste (wrapped in foil), 5 chopped red Asian shallots (eschalots), 1 finely chopped lemongrass stem (white part only), 1 tablespoon chopped galangal and 10 chopped garlic cloves. Unwrap the paste. Mix the chilli, roasted ingredients and ¼ teaspoon of ground cinnamon, ½ teaspoon ground nutmeg and ¼ teaspoon ground cloves to a smooth paste in a food processor, mortar and pestle or spice grinder. If the mixture is too dry, add a little vinegar to moisten it. Will keep in an airtight container in the refrigerator for up to 1 month.

Sri Lankan curry powder

MAKES ⅓ CUP

Dry-fry the following ingredients separately over low heat, until fragrant: 3 tablespoons coriander seeds, 1½ tablespoons cumin seeds, 1 teaspoon fennel seeds and ¼ teaspoon fenugreek seeds. It is important to do this separately as all spices brown at different rates. Make sure the spices are well browned, not burnt. Place the browned seeds in a food processor, blender or mortar and pestle, add a 2.5 cm (1 inch) cinnamon stick, 6 cloves, ¼ teaspoon cardamom seeds, 2 teaspoons dried curry leaves and 2 small dried red chillies and process or grind to a powder. Store in an airtight container in a cool, dry place.

Thai green curry paste

MAKES 1 CUP

Preheat the oven to 180°C (350°F/Gas 4). Put the following ingredients in a dish and bake for 5–10 minutes, or until fragrant: 1 teaspoon white peppercorns, 1 teaspoon cumin seeds, 2 tablespoons coriander seeds and 2 teaspoons shrimp paste (wrapped in foil). Unwrap the shrimp paste. Mix the above ingredients in a food processor or mortar and pestle, and add the following: 1 teaspoon of sea salt, 4 finely chopped lemongrass stems (white part only), 2 teaspoons chopped galangal, 2 teaspoons finely shredded makrut (kaffir lime) leaves, 1 tablespoon chopped coriander (cilantro) root, 5 chopped red Asian shallots (eschalots), 10 chopped garlic cloves, 16 chopped large green chillies. Mix all ingredients to a smooth paste. Keep in an airtight container in the refrigerator for up to 1 month.

Curry pastes

Thai red curry paste

MAKES 1 CUP

Preheat the oven to 180°C (350°F/ Gas 4). Soak 15 dried large chillies in boiling water for 10 minutes. Remove the seeds and roughly chop the flesh. Put 1 teaspoon white peppercorns, 2 teaspoons coriander seeds, 1 teaspoon cumin seeds and 2 teaspoons shrimp paste (wrapped in foil) in a dish and bake for 5–10 minutes, or until fragrant. Unwrap the shrimp paste. Mix the above ingredients in a food processor or mortar and pestle, and add the following: 5 red chopped Asian shallots (eschalots), 10 garlic cloves, 2 finely chopped stalks lemongrass (white part only), 1 tablespoon chopped galangal, 2 tablespoons chopped coriander (cilantro) root and 1 teaspoon finely grated makrut (kaffir lime) zest. Mix all ingredients to a smooth paste. Will keep in an airtight container in the refrigerator for 1 month.

Thai yellow curry paste

MAKES ½ CUP

Mix the following ingredients to a paste in a food processor, blender or mortar and pestle: 8 small green chillies, 5 roughly chopped red Asian shallots (eschalots), roughly chopped, 2 chopped garlic cloves, 1 tablespoon finely chopped coriander (cilantro) stem and root, 1 chopped stalk lemongrass, white part only, 2 tablespoons finely chopped galangal, 1 teaspoon ground coriander, 1 teaspoon ground cumin, ½ teaspoon ground turmeric, ½ teaspoon black peppercorns and 1 tablespoon lime juice. Will keep in an airtight container in the refrigerator for 1 month.

Vindaloo paste

MAKES ½ CUP

Place the following ingredients in a food processor: 2 tablespoons grated fresh ginger, 4 chopped garlic cloves, 4 chopped red chillies, 2 teaspoons ground turmeric, 2 teaspoons ground cardamom, 4 cloves, 6 peppercorns, 1 teaspoon ground cinnamon, 1 tablespoon ground coriander, 1 tablespoon cumin seeds and 125 ml (4 fl oz/½ cup) cider vinegar. Mix for 20 seconds, or until well combined and smooth. Refrigerate for up to 1 month.

Stir-fry sauces

Black bean sauce

SERVES 4–6

Place 2 teaspoons cornflour (cornstarch) and 125 ml (4 fl oz/½ cup) vegetable stock in a small bowl and blend together. Drain and rinse a 170 g (6 oz) tin of black beans, place in a bowl and lightly mash with a fork. Stir in the cornflour mixture, 1 tablespoon mushroom soy sauce, 2 teaspoons sugar and 2 crushed cloves garlic.

Chilli oyster sauce

SERVES 4–6

Place 1 teaspoon sesame oil, 2 crushed cloves garlic, 1 tablespoon grated fresh ginger, 2 finely chopped small red chillies, 4 sliced spring onions (scallions), 2 tablespoons mirin and 125 ml (4 fl oz/½ cup) vegetable oyster sauce in a bowl and stir together well.

Ginger oyster sauce

SERVES 4–6

Combine 2 teaspoons cornflour (cornstarch) and 2 teaspoons water. Add ½ cup (125 ml/ 4 fl oz) dry sherry, 1 chopped small red chilli, 1 tablespoon grated fresh ginger, ½ teaspoon sesame oil and 2 tablespoons vegetable oyster sauce and stir well.

Hoisin sauce

SERVES 4–6

Place 60 ml (2 fl oz/¼ cup) hoisin sauce, 2 tablespoons vegetable stock, 1 tablespoon vegetable oyster sauce and 1 tablespoon sweet chilli sauce in a small bowl and stir together.

Japanese dressing

SERVES 4–6

Place 10 dried shiitake mushrooms in a bowl and cover with 375 ml (13 fl oz/1½ cups) boiling water. Soak for 10 minutes. Drain, reserving 60 ml (2 fl oz/¼ cup) of the liquid, and cut the mushrooms in quarters. Place 80 ml (2½ fl oz/⅓ cup) Japanese soy sauce, 1 teaspoon grated fresh ginger, 80 ml (2½ fl oz/ ⅓ cup) mirin, 2 tablespoons sugar and the reserved liquid in a bowl. Add the mushrooms and stir together well.

Sake sauce

SERVES 4–6

Soak 10 g (¼ oz) sliced dried Chinese mushrooms in boiling water for 5 minutes. Drain and reserve 2 tablespoons of the liquid. Place 2 tablespoons sake, 2 tablespoons kecap manis, 1 tablespoon sweet chilli sauce, ½ teaspoon sesame oil, 1 small finely chopped red chilli, 2 teaspoons finely chopped lemongrass, 1 tablespoon lime juice, the mushrooms and the reserved liquid in a bowl and stir well.

Index

Index

Published by Bay Books, an imprint of Murdoch Books Pty Limited.

Murdoch Books Australia
Pier 8/9, 23 Hickson Road
Millers Point NSW 2000
Phone: + 61 (0) 2 8220 2000
Fax: + 61 (0) 2 8220 2558
www.murdochbooks.com.au

Chief Executive: Juliet Rogers
Publishing Director: Kay Scarlett

Project manager and editor: Paul O'Beirne
Design concept: Heather Menzies
Design: Heather Menzies and Jacqueline Richards
Photographer: Steve Brown
Stylist: Michelle Noerianto
Food preparation: Wendy Quisumbing
Introduction text: Leanne Kitchen
Production: Kita George

ISBN 978 1 74196 299 4

Printed by i-Book Printing Ltd.
PRINTED IN CHINA.
This edition published 2008.

IMPORTANT: Those who might be at risk from the effects of salmonella poisoning
(the elderly, pregnant women, young children and those suffering from immune deficiency diseases)
should consult their doctor with any concerns about eating raw eggs.

CONVERSION GUIDE: You may find cooking times vary depending on the oven you are using.
For fan-forced ovens, as a general rule, set the oven temperature to 20°C (35°F) lower than indicated in the recipe.

NUTRITION: The nutritional information given for each recipe does not include any accompaniments, such as rice or pasta,
unless they are included in the ingredients list. The nutritional values are approximations and can be affected by biological and
seasonal variations in foods, the unknown composition of some manufactured foods and uncertainty in the dietary database.
Nutrient data given are derived primarily from the official NUTTAB95 database.